THE GREAT PRESIDENT

Leadership and Decisive Actions

MARIE OTIGBA

I dedicate this book to my mum.
You left us on Mother's Day Phoebe Philomena Otigba
15 October 1937 – 22 March 2020.

CONTENTS

Author's Notes

Let me tell you who I am. I am Marie Otigba, British citizen, born in Newcastle upon Tyne if I may proudly add, resident of London, with no affiliation to the US whatsoever. Like most Britons I have always been aware of what goes on in the States and have visited there, most recently in 1996. I started to become interested in American history while carrying out research for a previous book, The Bishop Anyogu, when I discovered that my ancestors had been instrumental in stopping slavery following Abraham Lincoln's cotton embargo in 1863. That was the bulk of my knowledge and interest in the USA until one day, purely by chance, a video clip appeared on my social media timeline. It was by Ian Leslie of the New Statesman in June 2016:

"By the end of this campaign, I suspect Trump will regret ever having got into politics. Even if he only loses by a few points, his name will be permanently toxified..."

I remember thinking, 'That's a bit harsh.' But then he won. When the inauguration was aired across the UK, I was tempted to switch off...until I saw how solemn Michelle Obama and Hilary Clinton appeared due to the victory. Everyone from his opponents to mainstream media to the entire world seemed to hate Trump, appalled by the idea of him as the US President.

But why?

Speaking with my friends and family didn't yield much in the way of results (good luck explaining 'executive orders' to some people).

Essentially, a lot of what I heard back from people could be summarized as 'Trump is a racist'. Others figured I needed to change my approach when it came to taking in news.

The air was thick with Trump-hate – especially when it was announced that he would be visiting the United Kingdom – and I found myself put off by the bombardment of negative publicity. I remember walking to Trafalgar Square to get a look at the anti-Trump protest taking place. It was an incredible spectacle, made up of mostly weird demented-behaving people that made me wonder why this was the class and calibre of Trump-protestors.

This hostility to the US President interested me and in the months that followed, I researched posts, news reports, anything that would give me a proper understanding of the accusations made at him that wasn't marred by bias or prejudice. I learned very quickly that facts were being mishandled by President Trump's critics. I spent many nights shouting at the television or radio for not getting them straight. I took to using an Ishikawa decision tree to doodle the media headlines and accurately predict the outcomes of various media reports. Once I realised there was going to be no major change in how Trump was depicted, I stopped paying too much attention to the mainstream media which looked like it would be unable to relinquish its hatred and bias of Trump.

But the growing hatred for President Trump continued to fascinate me and I couldn't help digging deeper. What I saw, was a pattern; during key moments of crisis, his opponents on the Democratic Party side were side-tracked by indecision and indecisiveness while President Trump was focused on keeping his campaign promises, doing right by his fellow countrymen and working to make America the most powerful country in the world. What started as a fun-filled board game to pass the time eventually snowballed into the manuscript you now see before you, made up of materials intended to keep people informed while passing time during the COVID-19 lockdown and a game in development, to be released by November 2020.

Prior to the lockdown, President Trump's handling of the American employment crisis revealed that 6.2 million American citizens were facing unemployment in February 2020. By May, that number had grown to 20.5 million, prompting Trump to assure citizens that tackling the economic crisis would be a major focus of his ahead of the 2020 elections.

By the time you have finished reading this, I hope that I will have managed to put forward the obstacles and hurdles that President Trump has faced and the leadership and decisive actions he has taken to help his country while having to overcome powerful political forces backed by unscrupulous media. I present to you, our greatest ally, President Donald John Trump, the 45th and president of the United States.

1

INTRODUCTION

January 20 2017, inauguration day for the 45th president of the United States. Throughout a single week, there was one topic dominating all news outlets – Donald Trump was now the President of the United States. Many people were clearly disheartened by the news because the media had convinced them that Trump wouldn't win. This piqued my interest following our own media whirlwind following the EU Brexit referendum, which had seen not only a media misfire, but the loss of our prime minister.

Throughout the Presidential race, the mainstream media had seemed hell-bent on depicting Trump as racist, misogynistic, anti-black, anti-immigrant, anti-Muslim, anti-media, basically every form of bigot rolled into one. At one point, the polls had given Hillary Clinton an 83% chance of winning. When Trump parlayed his 17% chance into victory many Hilary-lovers raged at her loss.

Even the new First Lady wasn't spared. Several fashion commentators made note of how Melania Trump had copied her 'Madonna' blue outfit from Jackie Kennedy, said to have worn a similar outfit on the day of her husband's inauguration in January 1961... only for a swift Google search to reveal that Jackie had originally worn a dress and coat made of 'beige' wool crepe. I put this down to our BBC trying to spin sensational stories rather than focus on actual news. I had also laughed and shared posts about the FLOTUS plagiarising an old 2008 speech made by Michelle Obama, only to find out later that the accusations were based on only three word – "integrity", "compassion" and "intelligence" – the reasons for the overblown media reactions? I never felt so ashamed of myself soon after.

Trump's inaugural address offered a promise of putting America first, hoping to silence the sceptics.

"... American carnage across the country, inequality, abandoned factories 'like tombstones' and 'the crime and the gangs and the drugs.' We will make America strong again, wealthy again, proud again, safe again and, yes! Together we will make America great again."

It was an "America first" policy in all things:

'We've defended other nations' borders while refusing to defend our own,' he said. 'But that is the past. And now we are looking only to the future."

The hate from journalists continued all during 2017 and the attacks, mockery of the president, his family and members of his cabinet would define President Trump's administration for the next three years. I became aware of the alleged mistakes, misdeeds and scandals that were played out on the BBC, ITV and Sky news, most of which abruptly stopped being talked about once the actual facts about them became known. I used to just forget the storyline, and tended to miss the end of the "debacles" as a new story line about the President came up. I was still rather uninterested in the mostly diabolical reports about the President.

I spoke to several US-based friends, asking why the people had so many accusations about the new President, and with all the accusations why could they not investigate and have him removed because the accusations were simply too much. One retorted, "I don't know, can't you listen to the news?"

Another took the time to inform me that the President had a history of being racist, but declined to give me any examples. I was off work that day, so decided to Google search – what I immediately saw was the President with his 'black' girlfriend. I discounted that as a Photoshop-manipulated photograph. And then I saw further years old photographs of the president with Mohamed Ali, Michael Jackson, then Michael Jordan, Al Sharpton, then Whoopi Goldberg, Oprah Winfrey and then a report that he was honoured with the 1986 Ellis Island award for his work in the black community. All of which made me wonder how he could have become racist seemingly overnight, on the day he declared to run for office on June 16, 2015.

The more I researched, the more I began to realise the mainstream media had manipulation strategy;

- Publish or broadcast a negative story about President Trump.
- Count on the fact that people will not bother to fact check or research news reports to make up their own decisions.
- People tend to forget the actual facts that eventually emerge and as such can be easily manipulated.
- News accusations are usually dropped and the media move on to a new story line once the previous one has been proven to be a false dead-end lead.

As I began to realize that President Trump was the target of a concerted campaign to ruin his reputation and that his opponents on all sides seemed to be acting unscrupulously I became indignant and wanted to fight against it. I started to follow the main stream media and read up on the anti-trump followers' comments on social media. I began trying to make my own points started from posting correct versions of events, then sharing comments. I grew exhausted explaining to brick walls and finally decided to make my own direct signature responses, for example:

"Trump. Leadership and Decisive Actions. 2020 Get Ready for It".

I think it must have worked, considering the insults and compliments that arose from it.

However, there was still the problem of people forgetting events that happened. For instance many did not realise that Obama had authorised the use of cages for illegal immigrants as far back as 2013 – a good three years before Trump came into office. In spite of that, he got lacerated by both Democrats and the mainstream media with their 'gotcha' questions about detaining illegal immigrants.

The mainstream media seemed hell-bent on depicting Trump as a racist, misogynistic, anti-black and anti-immigrant, anti-Muslim, anti-media, basically every form of bigotry rolled into one. Of course, the polls had been obviously mistaken; given Hillary Clinton an 83% chance of winning, Trump had about 16%, leaving all Hilary-lovers raging at the loss to Trump.

Several fashion commentators made note of how the new First Lady had copied her 'Madonna' blue outfit from Jackie Kennedy, said to have worn a similar outfit on the day of her husband's inauguration in January 1961... only for a swift Google search to reveal that Jackie had originally worn a dress and coat made of 'beige' wool crepe. I put this down to our BBC trying to spin sensational stories rather than focus on actual news.

Trump's inaugural address offered a promise of putting America first, hoping to silence the sceptics. After all this time, people have still not gotten used to Trump. Hateful news was still being broadcast. I was still rather nonchalant as I had no intentions of visiting the US and had few friends and family in that part of the world.

"... American carnage across the country, inequality, abandoned factories 'like tombstones' and 'the crime and the gangs and the drugs.' We will make America strong again, wealthy again, proud again, safe again and, yes! Together we will make America great again." 'We've defended other nations' borders while refusing to defend our own,' he said. 'But that is the past. And now we are looking only to the future."

The hate from journalists continued into 2017 and the attacks, mockery of the president, his family and members of his cabinet would define President Trump's administration for the next three years. I became aware of the ploys, plans and patterns that were played out on the BBC, ITV and Sky news, most of which abruptly stopped being broadcast. I used to just forget the storyline, tended to miss the end of the debacles as a new story line about the president came up. I was still rather stoic and resigned after the mostly diabolical reports about the president. I spoke to several US-based friends, asking why the people had so many accusations about the new president, and with all the accusations why could they not investigate and have him removed because the accusations were simply too much. One retorted, "I don't know, can't you listen to the news?"

Another took the time to inform me that the president had a history of being racist, but declines to give me any examples. I was off work that day, so decided to

Google search – what I immediately saw was the president with his 'black' girl-friend. I discounted that as a Photoshop-manipulated photograph. And then I saw further year's old photographs of the president with Mohamed Ali, Michael Jackson, then Michael Jordan, Al Sharpton, then Whoopi Goldberg, Oprah Winfrey and then a report that he was honoured with the 1986 Ellis Island award for his work in the black community. All of which made me wonder how he could have become racist, which seemed to have happened overnight, and he became racist suddenly on the day he declared to run for office on June 16, 2015.

The more I researched, the more I began to realise the mainstream media's manipulation strategy;

- The people will not bother to fact check or research news reports to make up their own decisions.
- The people do forget and as such can be easily manipulated, even social media posts get forgotten.
- News accusations are usually dropped and moved on to a new story line once the previous one has been proven to be a false dead-end lead.

I then became active on social media, the key was to follow the main stream media and read up on the anti-trump followers' comments. Trying to make my point started from posting correct versions of events, then sharing comments, however, when I got weary explaining to brick walls, I became exhausted I simply decided to make my own direct signature response;

I think it must have worked, considering the insults and compliments that arose from it. However, there was still the problem of people forgetting events that happened – for instance many did not realise that Obama actually sanctioned and authorised the uses of cages for illegal immigrants as far back as 2013 – a good three years before Trump came into office but got lacerated by both Democrats and the mainstream media with their 'gotcha' questions.

My signature response only served to let all know that the fake news posted would have no impact on Trump winning the 2020 elections. Few people read past the last 20 comments posted because a question about a post would just repeat itself. By the middle of 2018, I had documented several attacks and the outcomes that helped me to stand my ground in defence of the president and to try to steer people into being better informed. The next four years of President Trump's administration covered in this book moved so quickly, as attacks almost overlapped continuously to the next, with the Democrats and their mainstream media that were critical of just about every action and sentence made by President Trump whilst distracting the people. The mainstream media no longer informed but were also vying to distract and deflect the people from getting a hold of what was being played out on an almost daily basis; from the Russian Investigation, spying on Trump's campaign, getting caught persecuting no one, right up to the Black Lives Matter riot.

Once the COVID-19 lockdown started, I began tracking various topics, ending up with up with a collection of US political current affairs with a touch of UK references that I had collated to follow the events as they unfolded; mainly from the Impeachment hoax to Operation Warp speed – I just had to stop somewhere.

The information and commentaries from various sources are abundant, apolitical to US politics and I am not even an American citizen.

What I hope to achieve with this book is to inform, inspire readers into researching news reports to make their own decision and help them to remember past events that never get reported, understanding and capturing the United States politics in simple English to provide the attention and focus to the goings on and hopefully look forward to the November 2020 elections.

In researching and writing this book, I have become informed and enlightened and hope that this book may even do the same for others.

2

THE GREAT PRESIDENT TRUMP

DONALD JOHN TRUMP was born on 14 June 1946 to billionaire parents. Raised in Queens, he was sent to a military school where he was exposed to many tough people, gaining a love of sports which led to him joining a wrestling team. At this early age, he learned a lot about leadership which prepared him for the constant fights with the media and the Democrats.

His original ambition was to into films after he had graduated in 1968 with high grades (a Bachelor of Science in Economics from the Wharton School and specialising in Finance, he ended up in real estate all of which exposed him to the framework of macro-environmental factors used in environmental scanning of the business world; the component of strategic management that may have defined his business and political background. He comes a lot wiser from his vast business experience which has made him highly adept, more experienced, and more connected with people than most. The American people have for their president a person that can almost accurately pre-empt and figure out how to react and how to respond to challenges. Before entering politics, he was a businessman and television personality. In 1971, he became president of family real estate business The Trump Organization with a portfolio of skyscrapers, hotels, casinos, and golf courses. Trump later produced and hosted The Apprentice, a reality television series just and decided to enter the 2016 presidential race as a Republican and defeated 16 other candidates in the primaries.

As such, when attacked from all angles, from the democrats to the mainstream media, they are attempting to take on a person with a heightened form of strategic awareness with past experience giving him the hindsight of 'an astute Onitsha trader'.

There was more to the accolade of being hailed the first 'black President', at a White House event. The accolade on social media also referred to his negotiation skills, likened to a typical Onitsha, Nigerian main market trader; that will negotiate to sell the River Niger sands to a man living down the river, using several negotiating strategies or will simply walk away from the negotiating process. He would bide his time listening and waiting and even get to fisticuffs by literally shamelessly stripping off his shirt and shoes to physically wrestle his agitators to submission in public.

In his own words which are more carefully calculated than they appear;

'...the fact that if you are right you've got to take a stand, or people will walk over all over you' as stated in his book, Trump: The Art of the Deal.

With political light years advantage, his opponents continue with their futile and defeatist assault on the President, who bides his time and then strikes back so hard – most of the time by his adversaries falling into their own traps. For those that still cannot understand how tough the president is – all I am trying to say here is, he will blend in easily in either Tottenham or Hackney straighten out crime and have the mayor of London hauled out with his ear, life-sized portrait and all.

Street talk, locker room talk, G20 Summits – he understands people and culture and can easily influence their views, their values, their humour, their hopes, their loyalties, and their worries and fears. His teenage years and business background exposed him to working with people and building relationships with them, which has helped him to have above average perspective and understanding of the diverse cultures of the USA – he is all about helping the American people, as stated in his World Economic Forum Davos address in January 2020;

"Now is the perfect time to bring your business, your jobs, and your investments to the United States of America."

Despite not being favoured in most forecasts by the mainstream media, he was elected over Democratic nominee Hillary Clinton, despite losing the popular vote. On winning, the outcry from the mainstream media and the Democrats was that Trump's policies meant that America would return to the period when America was racist, sexist, homophobic, and xenophobic. They added that his policies would erase all of the progress America has made since the civil rights struggles of the 1960s, and most disagreeable of all, being a former reality-TV star with ridiculous hair, he would lead the world into nuclear war.

The president's political positions have been described as populist, protectionist, and nationalist, emphasized by his campaign slogan – Make America Great Again – MAGA.

Trump is rather eloquent especially at his rallies where he is with his army of supporters and just about every word and sneeze of the president is put under the microscope of the press.

The supporters love the captivating rallies which have made many previously unaffected people change from a very neutral standpoint to becoming proud 'deplorables'.

UK'S STRONGEST ALLY AND LEADER OF THE FREE WORLD

The president's US support base are fundamentally attracted to the president's charisma; he has his very own style of showmanship, as seen in news briefings, on the podiums and in his rallies, strengthened in notoriety from being in 14 seasons of the very successful show The Apprentice.

Many have seen him in terms of the rational, leadership decisions that he made during the show and can see the person that became president not with the financial backings of the powerful king makers as every other president has, but by being himself and as such answerable to none.

But this does not apply to most of his UK support base that lacked knowledge of him until the inordinate negative hateful media reports brought him to their attention. The excess of tripe definitely aroused my attention. We used to regard the mainstream media BBC and ITV as highly respected for accuracy and objectivity, however, in the past five years, from around 2015, they have failed to provide fair coverage and the British silent majority saw through it all, bided their time and then hammered them at the right time – as the world saw during the Brexit referendum when the whole of Europe woke up to such a shuddering shock.

I began to notice the BBC bias from watching Question Time. What became obvious was that in the panel audience of five, only one would speak out for the president, and whenever the person spoke out, the other panel members and audience overwhelmed the Trump supporting speaker rather angrily.

This prejudice by the UK mainstream media has persisted and it was no surprise that someone set up a Facebook chat group 'I Hate BBC Question Time'. I then decided to give up on BBC TV news and settled for only BBC Radio 4. However, within a few months, Jonathan Dimbleby left in early 2019 and so did John Humphrys. I did struggle to what was being sludged on air and purely by chance stumbled on Leading British Conversation (LBC) – which was even worse as far as the president was concerned. But then, I began to use their broadcast to provide materials for my analysis of current affairs and hence this book.

Despite the UK being America's strongest ally, Obama had chosen then-Japanese Prime Minister Taro Aso as his first foreign visitor to the Oval Office but our former prime Minister Theresa had received an invitation to be the first guest to the White House after Trump got elected on 27 Jan 2017.

Obama had threatened that if we voted for Brexit and that the UK will be forced to the back of the queue for any trade negotiations; which excited the mainstream media, the EU countries and the UK 'remainers' everywhere – I did not hear the last of Obama's threat, which seemed directed at me. Many 'remainers' were silent, and at the time, I had thought that I was the only 'remainer' in the whole of the UK.

The 'Brexiteers' calmly and quietly kept their cool – we were all going to bide our time, but then we woke up to a shocking victory, we had won – decorum and decency meant pretending to look as subdued as the losers – but we all knew ourselves – with our sudden occasional wide manic grin.

In contrast to Obama, President Trump had a keen interest in talking up a trade deal with the UK, so Trump came across as being our strong ally and I intended to show it by waving an American flag when he visited.

The hurt was as deep as their hate because four years on, the 'remainers' and media have still not gotten over losing. The UK was still in the turbulent pre-Brexit period when Trump had decided to visit the UK. The pattern of bile hate continued right through and intensified when Air Force One stormed through the clouds to the United Kingdom.

The mainstream media in the USA and the UK are mostly anti-Trump, and they hate his election slogan 'Make America Great

Again' (MAGA), which does not target any race, gender, sociological or socioeconomic group. Instead, it was meant to unify the Americans, to come together in support of the essence of the United States of America and it was obvious that other campaigns (especially the Democrats) made particular appeals to various groups, and used divisive hate language. Hence the exaggerated venom came from only the liberals, as I experienced during his first visit to the UK as president – where we were literally escorted, penned in and protected from the aggressive, well-organised anti-Trump crowd.

TRUMP'S VISIT TO THE UK

The negative media report reverberated when Trump's state visit to the United Kingdom was scheduled. A state visit to the UK is one of the highest honours it can bestow on a visiting statesman, and protests on both mainstream media and social media were stoking hate and calling people out to protest. The United Kingdom have previously invited and hosted absolute despotic heads of states from Asia and Africa so when London's mayor Sadiq Khan, called for the invitation to be rescinded, that got me on Ebay and Amazon looking to be kitted out in full MAGA gear to welcome Trump at Trafalgar Square.

The mayor as everyone would agree is a very irritating incompetent person. So when Khan decided to use Trump's visit and the media frenzy to his advantage, I immediately wrote to the President, with a copy to the mayor himself, urging the president to help me in exposing his incompetence to the world.

The UK is not Trump's jurisdiction, however, Khan had announced that he was intending to cordon off the roads to prevent Trump supporters from gathering. He had announced that the roads were going to be cordoned off to allow only the well organised, sponsored anti-Trump protestors on the streets. There were no provisions for Trump supporters and I stated in my letter that preventing Trump supporters from coming out to wave was in the president's interest and an infringement of my rights to welcome him.

The three days before the visit, I had given up on all the ITV news channels. The BBC including 'Question time' and Andrew Marr, were relentless with their new style interviewing tactics picked up from the American media of continually interrupting throughout the interview, with the aim to give the audience only their views in the form of questions and blocking the chance for the audience to hear the responses.

The news coverage went on about the Trump blimp, a puerile airborne effigy of the president, approved by the mayor of London, which they were all happy to report was 'ready to be floated over London'.

The media had taken over every aspect of the media with that asinine blimp– It seemed like there was no other news to report.

The US president then used a bombshell interview ahead of his UK visit to chastise and berate Khan over the wave of terror attacks in the capital.

Mr Khan questioned why he was singled out as being responsible for terrorism –if only Khan had bothered to read my mail, I had clearly stated that he was an annoying incompetent twerp that could not cope with the crime rate and that many, including me, were going to lose our jobs because of him making us late for work.

The city had just experienced the most gruesome terror attack only hours before the President touched down in the UK, however, that was quickly swept under the carpet and prominence was given to the blimp. The president followed the interview with a tweet;

"At least 7 dead and 48 wounded in terror attack," and Mayor of London says there is 'no reason to be alarmed!"

During the interview, I was so pleased that the President responded with absolute venom especially when he further went on to call Khan a 'stone cold loser' – I had been avenged.

The visit had created so much outrage that it ended up being debated in

Parliament. By the time President Trump finally touched down in the UK for his first official visit since becoming US president, my MAGA cap from Amazon had arrived, and the country was braced with Trump frenzy. We were not disappointed. He stormed in as what seemed to be a whirlwind to the United Kingdom with FLOTUS Melania on Air Force One fresh from that NATO summit in Brussels. Being his first official visit, on day one, I was one of the inquisitive people that came out to Westminster Abbey to experience the commotion. Trumped up, I got to Victoria and walked past Westminster Cathedral to get to Westminster Abbey.

The roads were all cordoned off and blocked up, but there I was with some 300 supporters and of course the Metropolitan police that had used their cars to create four layers of car defence wall.

As we chatted to each other excitedly about being hopefully able to catch a glimpse through the police cordon and in general discussed the excessive media attacks, a black reporter, microphone in hand and her cameraman tailing made a beeline at me. She introduced herself as a reporter from the Guardian newspaper and angrily wanted to 'know why a black woman would come out on the street, with a MAGA cap and a small US flag to welcome the president and'– before I would have the chance to reply another Trump supporter butted in; "Madam, you do realise that that is a racist question?"

That cheered up the crowd around me as she quietly moved on. Until then, I had not realised that it was offensive to the media to have the Trump hat on and that the UK were becoming like the US where the left-leaning media had to be very aggressive and hostile towards whoever did not agree with their views. They just get angry! They simply do not like you even being neutral or sitting on the fence. They do not tolerate diversity and inclusion unless you play or sing to their tune unconditionally. You are not allowed to express a point, they simply become so deranged with anger. Best of all is when their anger backfires and they are forced to see the point that was made earlier – they just shut down and never apologise or admit that they were wrong.

Despite the full-blown organised protests, the June 2017 visit went ahead and all those that intended to benefit by increasing their 'media profile' from their negative comments all had full media coverage of their twaddle against the president. As the silent majority sat and watched, all that was on our minds and social media posts was a speed-up to Election Day.

The media was relentless with their continual anti-Trump frenzy after the tweet, which got me fired out to Trafalgar Square the next day, fully Trumped up with an American flag and of course my MAGA cap, where many people shook our hands, some took our photographs and commented with words of encouragement and absolute guts.

I declined all interviews with the press – I knew better than that and I was not there for a photo opportunity.

The police would not let us go any further – but it was great strutting about proudly with our MAGA caps and US flag, 'safely' behind the police cordon – which enraged the crowd as they could not get to us physically – but taunted 'your hat is made in China' at us.

We were soon joined by some plain clothes 'Trumpers' in the pen. Some did not know where to purchase the Trump gear and others stated that they were not that fanatical to get 'Trumped' up.

The next day was a Saturday and my usual lazy TV-couch day was going to be spent at the American Embassy across the Thames. I met up with some 500 Trump supporters and we all marched across the Lambeth Bridge to Whitehall.

We were stopped by the police that had cordoned off the road – It soon looked as if the riot police were getting into formation and that was my cue to backtrack – smack into the hands of another police cordon. Here, I argued that I was merely an ordinary Trump supporter and insisted on walking past the cordon but was immediately carried out of the way by the riot police.

We backtracked to another police cordon, and pleaded that I had had enough and wanted to go home. I was then advised that the only way I could go safely home was to merge with the tourists and on-lookers to get to Charing Cross underground station and then home and that I had to do something about my top and to abandon my 'Trump is Our Number 1 Ally' placard. They allowed me some privacy in their van to wear my top inside out and the US flag was now rolled over, tucked in my bag with the white handle sticking out. I soon re-joined the Trump supporters whilst pretending to be a 'timid tourist'.

By around 2pm, the protesters' numbers now swelled with climate activists ('Extension Rebellion'), not to mention pro-abortionists most of whom looked rather confused with glazed looks. Our number had also swelled as we were joined by some 5000 strong 'Tommy Robinson' supporters. I had physically had

"You know it does not really matter what the media write."

The best taco bowls are made in Trump Tower Grill. I love the Hispanics."

"Whenever one of the morons says I wear a wig, stop reading because they have no credibility and just hate."

"They, and the 'Lame stream Media' (including Jake), have spent three and a half years illegally smearing me. They got caught!"

Rand Paul – 'I never attacked him on his looks, and believe me, there's plenty of subject matter right there.

"...stone cold loser"

"I was very excited to receive this invitation and ruin your evening in person. That's why I accepted."

On former chief strategist Steven Bannon: "That guy leaked more than the Titanic."

"I just want to say this, this is one of the best times I've had with the media — this might be the most fun I've had since watching your faces on election night."

"You would have chosen not to contribute to the Clinton foundation. She talks about me being dangerous, she has killed many thousands of people with her stupidity"

On Arianna Huffington;

"@arianahuff is unattractive both inside and out. I fully understand why her former husband left her for a man – he made a good decision."

"If Hillary Clinton can't satisfy her husband what makes her think she can satisfy America?"

"The only card she has is the woman's card. She's got nothing else to offer and frankly, if Hillary Clinton were a man, I don't think she'd get 5 percent of the vote. The only thing she's got going is the woman's card, and the beautiful thing is, women don't like her."

"What a stupid question that is – you ask a lot of stupid questions. First of all the good news is not a lot of people listen to your radio show"

"You talk about dog walking and washing dishes – and the world is listening instead on asking proper questions that is stupid. You are a really stupid person"

On Global Warming;

"It's really cold outside today, they are calling it a major freeze, weeks ahead of normal. Man, we could use a big fat dose of global warming!"

"I say, not in a braggadocious way, I've made billions and billions of dollars dealing with people all around the world."

"To be blunt, people would vote for me. They just would.

Why? Maybe because I'm so good looking."

"You're going to win so much you may get tired of winning."

"The line of 'Make America great again,' the phrase, that was mine, I came up with it about a year ago, and I kept using it, and everybody's using it, they are all loving it. I don't know, I guess I should copyright it, maybe I have copyrighted it."

"The concept of shaking hands is absolutely terrible, and statistically I've been proven right."

"I think the big problem this country has is being politically correct. I've been challenged by so many people and I don't, frankly, have time for total political correctness."

"Are you going to apologize, Yahoo?"

"That's why you're Yahoo and nobody knows who the hell you are."

"North Korea best not make any more threats to the United States. They will be met with fire and fury like the world has never seen."

"...healing not hatred...Justice not Chaos...Security not Anarchy are the mission..."

"...you cannot be number one on earth if you cannot be number One in Space."

"You mean Pompeo is under investigation for someone walking his dog? Here is a man negotiating war and peace and all you are interested in is walking his dog? This country's media has a long way to go... the priorities are all screwed up.... dog walking and washing dishes. What you are asking me is so terrible, it's so stupid – you know how stupid that sounds to the world?"

Reader, when the president calls one 'stupid', it is meant to be an insult—no other way to spin it. It's a real hard-hitter, and Trump is not shy of hard-hitting.

PAVING THE ROUTE TO A TRUMP DYNASTY

Max Weber, the philosopher and sociologist studies provided us with three types of authorities that make a leader; Traditional, Legal-Rational, and Charismatic; each of which correspond to a form of leadership that operate in a contemporary society, with "legitimacy being common aspect in all three because a legitimate authority is justified by both the ruler and the ruled.

President Trump fits squarely with a mix of Legal Rational and larger doses of Charismatic authority and strategy when performing his job, which many people like.

The key strategy that Trump used for the 2016 campaigns was to ignore the states that could have pulled him the popular votes and instead, focused hard on the swing cash cow rich delegate college states. The rather laid-back Democrats relied on their propaganda mainstream media arm to belch out distorted polls, quite unlike the Republicans that relied mainly on only social media and Trump's electrifying rallies to inform his base.

This strategy left Clinton exposed to Trump. For instance, her conventions were dominated by black women but very few were represented in her policies; for instance, the car affordability scheme of June 2016 which was not within the reach of her black woman demographics. In fact, the scheme made new cars un-affordable for black people.

In effect, the post-electoral stress disorder from losing to Trump generated a hysteria still manifesting after three years with a series of hateful accusations; the Russian investigations, the Ukrainian Investigations and the impeachment hoax frame up to remove the president.

For all its vacuity, their lack of thought and lack of intelligence made their hysteria understandably intense and nefarious because Trump has continued do what he promised; defying all expectations. Also, the Black voter pre-ordained fealty to the Democratic Party is dwindling, although many make up part of Trump's 'silent majority'. In 2016, had journalists and observers done some less-biased research they may have determined that there were a host of silent supporters lurking around the voting booths, despite leading commentators asserting that Trump was unelectable. The democrat strategists failed to recognise the centrality of identity politics and persisted on talking about the rich and poor instead of the social-groups of African Americans, Hispanics, native-Americans, Aleuts, Asian Americans, LGBT Americans, and even 'Euro-Americans' – the president's strategy here was to highlight the issues relating to the various groups and how he intended to rectify them.

The Democrats made more mistakes and still do. They are extremely villainous and personal, highlighting only his personality, and despise Trump for his blue-collar tastes in everything from his hair-style to his food; relishing the junk of Domino's, KFC and McDonalds with large fries, the faux pas offenses. They also get deranged with his impulsively vulgar but accurate responses to mainstream media's 'gotcha' questions.

While Obama had dedicated his last days in office strangling industries such as the motor industries and hatching out plots to take out the new president, Trump was already gearing up to revoke most of Obama's policies within a week of getting into the White House, as he had promised during his rallies, including exposing the mass exclusion of Americans from not only new car ownership as a result of wage stagnation but also from world trade.

Another huge mistake was to label Trump supporters as; "deplorables – beer drinking, gun-owning, TV-watching, church-going, cigarette-smoking class who would prefer to hold on to dying or dead coal mining jobs, oil drilling assembly line motor jobs and not embrace fashion designing or other creative roles like FX trading and software engineering."

Trump went directly for the attack on these labels, he promised to bring back industries that were operating abroad, and would open up coal mines.

The working class far outnumbered the blue collared rich few so when Trump claimed that he was working for the American people, the numbers reflected Trump's win.

In his 2016 inaugural speech, Trump warned that the country was very grim and that he would not forget the mass American people that were not driving around in brand new cars or their pressing immediate needs, which included restricting cheap labour inflows mostly from Mexico unless they come in legally and most important of all. Although they are mostly gardeners, cleaners, Filipino child minders, Asian chefs, dog walkers Indian software programmers –which are the American pseudo-elite – the Hollywood actors strongly objected to this because they selfishly saw the cost of employing their cheap labour rise. However, the crowding effect meant that the legal immigrants that did those jobs on that wage also suffered.

Backed with a $1.3 trillion budget plan for infrastructure Trump seemed to be coasting into a 2020 re-election especially if the Mexican border gets sealed off. The president promised to legalise all the tax-paying and non-felonious illegal immigrants which would give him a chunk of the Hispanic votes – after failed promises by Obama – this was never aired on mainstream media.

As a businessman, he would play his hand and lock in the opposition. The opposition have held that he has been made bankrupt several times in response. This is fake news, we see a president never filed for personal bankruptcy, but a person that managed to weather the knocks of the recession that engulfed most business during the nineties. My research confirmed that even Abraham Lincoln failed 25 times as a politician before he became president – so when he got to the place of blessing, he knew how to handle it.

Although disrespecting the flag, the police or any one of the armed forces is guaranteed to gain a direct onslaught from the president, anything else, he will bide the time and he almost seems to thrive on being attacked and many have cited that he mischievously plants the seeds of attacks, and when he retaliates, it hits you out with the most amazing blow, and the frightening thing of all is that you do not see it coming.

From experience comes his proactive 'hunch' and intuitive nature, gained from years of liaison with teams of lawyers, reading tiny prints, checking and negotiating deals – all of which he does as second nature. He easily predicts opponents' moves and uses various tactical backup alternatives to deliver his objectives.

Most of President Trump's supporters claim that they are not interested in his personal life, which both the Democrats and the mainstream media may have now realised, because that line of attack seems to have dwindled as they are being exposed on a daily basis.

The supporters love that President Trump does not take the nonsense put out by the media and does get things done. Several of his supporters, if not all his supports continue to affirm that; "...he may be imperfect in his personal life, but is perfect for the job."

Donald Trump is neither sponsored by any special interest nor is he sponsored by a financial backer, which makes him a thorough leader through and through.

The supporters greatly admire that President Trump earns only

$1 dollar per annum because refusing to earn his income is a violation of the constitution; so he deliberately earns a dollar and donates his remaining $399 thousand dollars to charity every quarter, which means he will be TAX-FREE throughout his term as President of the United States. No American President has ever done it!!

HE KNOWS WHERE THE BODIES ARE BURIED

From the day of his inauguration – the democrats had already decided to impeach Trump. From my research, I realised that from the day that he decided to run for office, hardly anyone thought that he could win. I found footage after footage of Hollywood celebrities, TV personalities, and political commentators voicing their confidence that Trump would never be president.

Trump would have to be up against Clinton, a political figurehead – loved by the elite Hollywood, her billionaire sponsors, and of course, the sycophant media. There are several Hollywood celebrities in a video clip whom I still love to watch over and over again, because of the disappointment that they were later to experience. That clip starts with Trump saying;

"Nice guys, shame about their views but I like them."

In one clip celebrity host, John Oliver stares at the camera saying,

"Do it, do it. Look at me, do it, I will personally write you a campaign check now on behalf of this country who do not want you to be president, but who badly want you to run."

An MSNBC host commented,

"...if I were Hilary Clinton right now, I will be thinking of how big I will win. Even if Donald Trump wins most of the states – he will still lose from the Electoral College...

his race as of tonight is no longer a presidential race, the race is over, he might as well accept the question on how does he minimise damage...as far as Donald Trump is concerned, it will never, ever, happen..."

In another clip, Bernie Sanders screamed, to the cheers of his supporters,

"...Donald Trump will not be President..."

We then see Pelosi,

"...he is not going to be president, Donald Trump is never going to be president of the United States, take it to the bank, and I guarantee it...'

In a jibe with Trump there in the audience, the host continues,

"...Donald Trump says he is running for President of the United States, which is surprising, because I thought he was running as a joke... I love you Donald Trump, but there is zero chance we will see you being sworn in with your hands on the golden bible."

Ann Hart Coulter, a best-selling author was jeered at by the host of the show when she predicted that '...*Trump could win...*'

Shamelessly, Obama joined in, "...I may go down as the worst president of the United States! ... but at least I will go down as a president"

Another celebrity pundit Nate Silver predicted a Hillary Clinton win of 50 to 38.

Then Stephen Colbert implored Trump,

"...you're not going to be president, alright. It's been fun. It's been great, but come on, buddy..."

The vilification and disrespect increased – but what came across was that he seemed to be basking in their insults – he came back with that swagger and poise, now used on the podium and then he did that smile with a body language that said, "Watch me – I will be President."

And it would take more than taunts and goading to floor or embarrass Trump. If only they had bothered to read about his early years. What they still cannot see is a common-sense pragmatic person who was not bought and has nothing to sell but giving back to the country that he loves – and cannot be influenced by lobbyists.

The Democrats do not communicate their policies except hate and vent, meanwhile, the president remains confident and unscathed, and it seems certain that he knows where the Democrats have buried all the proverbial bodies ...and how the bodies got there!

It also seems that it's a Trump dynastic likelihood that the democrats are rabid about and not Trump. Ivanka Trump is seen at an international meeting with President Trump and is duly apprenticed in the White House and is beginning to look credible to occupy that seat as America's first female president in 2024.

3

PRESIDENT DONALD TRUMP IS RACIST

This whole chapter was burned out when my research produced details that Trump had actually dated a black lady for over two years.

4

PROMISES MADE AND PROMISES KEPT

The executive branch is headed by the president and is formally independent of both the legislature and the judiciary. The executive branch is a vast organisation numbering about four million people, including one million active-duty military personnel. In addition to Vice president Michael R. Pence, the president is surrounded with a world-class cabinet such as Attorney General William Pelham Barr. President Trump made a string of promises during his long campaign and they all know the parts to play. I have managed to research the key achievements that never made it to the mainstream media, or were not fully covered;

THE WALL

Every country in the world had border controls. Even the United Kingdom, the most tolerant country in the world, has border controls, however, the Democrats have decided to have a free for all open border in the United States and have continually attacked the president for building border walls, little did I know that the walls and fencing built under the 2006 act was not the first border fencing in the United States. The US Border Patrol first began to erect physical barriers in its San Diego sector in 1990 and the fourteen miles of fencing approved by President George H. W. Bush was erected along the border of San Diego,

California, and Tijuana, Mexico – yet the mainstream media accused Trump of being racist for reinforcing the old wall.

The Democrats want open borders merely for illegal immigrants to come in and swell up the number of people to vote for them, they are not thinking ahead of the impact of mass free for all immigration on the economy.

ILLEGAL IMMIGRANTS

While figures showed that illegal border crossings had seen an overall decline since 2000, they began rising again around 2012 and around 2015, border patrol staff were beginning to face 'unprecedented border security and humanitarian crises' along the southwest border.

Drugs coming into the US posed another huge problem in the US, with over 70% of heroin coming from across the southern border which the wall would help to fight, the next problem was undocumented persons.

Being undocumented has significant practical, social and economic impacts and permeates the everyday lives of the people.

Being undocumented often creates a transitory and insecure identity. Lack of status is an all-encompassing experience, producing distinctive forms of social marginality with significant impacts such as 'enforced' mobility to avoid detection and even death, hence the reasons to come in through the 'front door' like many other migrants from south and Central America.

Throughout his 2016 presidential campaign, Trump called for the construction of a much robust border wall, claiming that if elected, he would 'build the wall and make Mexico pay for it.'

The then-President of Mexico Enrique Peña Nieto said that his country would not pay for any such wall. The issue of how to pay for the wall caused a stand-off within Congress and as usual, the Democrats as expected would oppose any of the presidents' policies – no matter how beneficial to their people and as such, refused to approve money for the project and they paid protesters to campaign along the wall with their placards screaming 'Illegal Immigrants are Welcome'.

In March 2019, the first funds for the wall were given the goahead. A total of $1 billion (about £758 million) was authorised by the Pentagon – the US department in charge of both the National

Security and the American military forces and the president managed to raise $22.2 million from the $5.6 billion needed.

As things always fall into President Trump's advantage, Mexican President Andrés Manuel López Obrador was elected in December 2018.

In May 2019, Trump threatened to hit all Mexican exports with tariffs unless Mr López Obrador cracked down on the surge of migrants arriving at the US border. Mexico caved in right away, probably after they saw China losing the trade war against President Trump.

Mexico then diverted thousands of its new National Guard police to deter migrants at Mr Trump's behest. The result was a 75% drop in migrant arrests at the US border.

Mexico had rejected payment for the construction project as out of the question, but by October 2019, Mexico had agreed albeit indirectly to pay the $5.7 billion the president wanted for the wall, the reason for this was that it ceased the Mexicans' problems;

"Given the dramatic increase in migrants moving from Central America through Mexico to the United States, both countries recognize the vital importance of rapidly resolving the humanitarian emergency and security situation."

Trump's stance on border security had initially prevented vulnerable women and children from being trafficked, and then came the coronavirus pandemic which got Congress screaming that President Trump was not building the wall quick enough to limit people coming in from countries with a high propensity of coronavirus and that he was being very slow to act. Not only that, as recent as 21 June 2020, three individuals from terror-sponsoring Iran were detained and arrested at the southern border. Again, here, Trump was right – terrorists posed a potential threat at the borders.

With figures correlating to crime, human trafficking and employment in the US, as far as the Democrats and main stream media were concerned, they hoped that the Americans people will forget and indeed they did forget that Obama had deported more undocumented workers than any other president in history.

DEFERRED ACTION FOR CHILDHOOD ARRIVALS (DACA)

Many children over the past years have come into the US with or without their parents, some on a holiday visa and decided to stay on or simply crossed the borders – Deferred Action for Childhood Arrivals (DACA) refers to those that have not even claimed some form of asylum. In effect, like in all developed countries globally, they are undocumented and as the months turn into years, have no legal status.

(DACA) is the American immigration policy set up by the Obama administration that allows these undocumented individuals that came in as children to receive a renewable two-year period of deferred action from deportation and become eligible for a work permit in the US – depending on what sort of work they seek, could greatly affect the employment numbers of American citizens seeking work.

President Trump declared that the order was a 'totally illegal document' and that the former president never had the right to sign the executive order because it shielded the so-called "Dreamers" from deportation and provided work and study permits to the detriment of American citizens that needed work. The Trump administration announced a "wind-down" of the scheme, that was a tactical move with foresight because the coronavirus made over 20 million unemployed which justified his stance on DACA.

The president had stated that, "Obama never had the legal right to sign DACA. But In any event, how can he have the right to sign and I don't have the right to 'unsigned."

An analysis from Immigration Law Institute's Christopher Hajec also called the program 'unlawful.'

The Supreme Court is still to decide whether the Trump administration can end this illegal DACA program.

The DACA programme affects an estimated 700,000 young people who entered the US without documents as children.

'Dreamers' are looked on more favourably than those that come in through the 'back door' and the same Dreamers feel entitled because they are higher up the pecking order than the illegal immigrants.

The president's main focus was on the undocumented immigrants and the children who at best would be exploited and at worse, murdered by their criminal traffickers.

Trump, who campaigned on repealing DACA in 2016, announced a plan in 2017 to phase out the program, but was blocked by federal courts that ruled that the phase-out could not apply retroactively and that the program should be restarted.

The White House fought back on those decisions, saying that 'the President has broad authority over immigration enforcement policy.' The Supreme Court rejected President Donald Trump's effort to end legal protections for 650,000 young illegal immigrants, for now, those immigrants are still protected from deportation and their authorization to work in the United States.

Depending on who is saying it, over the past decades, the Americans have always had the same immigration policy and solution to open borders.

As far back as President Clinton's administration, Clinton had decided to hire twice as many border patrol guards to secure the borders and deport more of the illegal aliens than before.

Even Bernie Sanders had felt that since property prices were increasing and wages going down, he did not think it right for people to come in as guest workers, to apply and obtain work on lower wages, which had the effect of driving wages down for many US workers.

In 2005, Obama did not want them pouring in to the US undetected, undocumented, unchecked and jumping the queues over those in queues waiting patiently and diligently to get their immigration papers legally.

Furthermore, video evidence showed Obama confirming that it was not right for children to arrive through the US southern borders, unaccompanied and illegally most of whom arrived through sex traffickers.

The problem here as well was that there was no way of tracking the children – most shocking of all, many children did not make the journey and forensic evidence showed that some were even killed.

Hilary Clinton had urged Mexico to do more to prevent the influx of the immigrants and she wanted them deported for any transgressions of any kind.

In 2009, US Senate Democratic Leader Chuck Schumer stated that illegal immigration was wrong 'pure and simple' and until it was restricted the US would make no progression dealing with illegal immigration.

In effect, the Democrats all knew that open borders were critical issues, they all talked about it but could do nothing about it – and then came Trump!

Hollywood, the democrats and mainstream media – including our BBC decided that Trump's political promise on the wall was racists.

As expected, they spent the first term of President Trump harshly criticising each sentence – the democrat's manipulation tool again was in place – 'the people do forget' and as such can be easily manipulated.

Here are statements made by Obama which 90% of Democrats and their liberal supporters will not know he had made:

"It's important to recognize two things. Firstly, the surge of unaccompanied children, and adults with children, are arriving at one sector of the border, and that's the Rio Grande Valley. Secondly, the issue is not that people are evading our enforcement officials. The issue is that we're apprehending them in large numbers.

"While we intend to do the right thing by these children, their parents need to know that this is an incredibly dangerous situation and it is unlikely that their children will be able to stay. And I've asked parents across Central America not to put their children in harm's way in this fashion

"Right now, there are more border patrol agents and surveillance resources on the ground than at any time in our history. And we deport almost 400,000 migrants each year... and earlier this week, Mexico announced a series of steps that they're going to take on their southern border to help stem the tide of these unaccompanied children.

"...the Senate passed a common-sense, bipartisan bill more than a year ago. It would have strengthened the border, added an additional 20,000 border patrol agents. It would have strengthened our backlogged immigration courts. It would have put us in a stronger position to deal with this surge and, in fact, prevent it.

"Right now, kids who come to the border from Mexico are immediately deported, but because it's non-contiguous, folks who are coming from Central America have to go through a much lengthier process... but also to make sure that we're sending a strong signal that they can't simply show up at the border and automatically assume that they're going to be absorbed."

Obama's speech clearly confirms that the problem long existed before Trump and the Democrats have relied on the fact that because many things happen- people forget as they re-focus on new events.

Leaving children in 'cages' while they awaited being processed was another Obama policy that the Democrats and the media ignored until several months into president Trump's administration.

In July 2018, there was Trump hysteria when the media went rabid with at- tacks on the president for caging up immigrant children.

The story behind this went as far back as 2012, when parents were sending their children unaccompanied to the US, and most of the time, the children were sexually abused without their parents at hand – and worse- many never made the journey into the US alive. In order to protect the children, Obama had separated them from the adults – some of whom claimed were the children's parents but indeed were not. It was for the children's protection if anything else as stated by Obama.

A 2014 photograph of Obama's Homeland Security Secretary, Jeh Johnson, was soon published showing him touring a facility in Arizona, in which the fencing could be clearly seen surrounding migrant children was splashed over the media – to show to people that the cages were set up by Obama.

That picture was taken during a spike in the number of unaccompanied children from Central American countries. However, Trump decided to change another Obama policy and set about immediately uniting children with family members in the adult centres.

Trump's former acting US Immigration and Customs Enforcement (ICE) director, Thomas Homan who was also Director at ICE under the former ad- ministration went on to comment that,

"...the kids are being housed in the same facility built under the former administration. If you want to call them cages, call them cages. But if the left wants to call them cages and the Democrats want to call them cages, then they have to accept the fact that they were built and funded in 2015."

MOTOR INDUSTRY

Trump's main problem with the motor industry was that many cars were imported into the United States and few countries wanted to import or buy American cars. Here in England, we tend to see those Hummers and Limousines as rather unsuitable for our rather narrow streets and not as stylish as our Mini's, Aston Martins or Rolls Royce or Bentleys anyway.

Another problem that the president faced was car manufacturing of American cars and the components outside the states. During the presidential campaign, Donald Trump took several shots at Ford, General Motors and Toyota for manufacturing outside the United States. Fiat Chrysler Automobiles managed to avoid Trump's attack by announcing a $1 billion investment in US plants to build Jeeps and pickups.

As the months went by numerous industry executives began to feel that in fact, the President could be great for the car business, because of the tax issues that bothered the motor manufacturers;

- Trump promising a corporate tax break that would be great for the automakers' bottom profit margin and
- The threatened border tax for importing foreign-made vehicles and foreign-made vehicle components into the US, such as the decision to impose a 35% import tax on all cars built in Mexico and imported into the US.

Mexico had experienced a considerable boom in its car industry, as manufacturers took advantage of cheaper labour and ease of trade access into the US. With incredible foresight – then came COVID-19 and many began to see the importance of having the US plants based in the United States.

The president used his selective use of tariffs with Europe to reinforce his made-in-America policy priority. He was elected on the platform of 'Make America Great Again.' For him that meant manufacturing and reclaiming America's pride of place for manufacturing, where the president felt America had been losing out.

Even companies that don't cite Trump's agitation are moving his way on the jobs question. An Italy-based brake manufacturer, which employs about 800 people in manufacturing operations in Homer, Michigan confirmed that,

"If you're close to suppliers and they're reasonably competitive, we think any difference in cost can be made up quickly by logistics and transportation advantages."

Also, Mexico, a member of the US-Mexico-Canada (USMCA) increasingly fills in for Chinese supply as a low-cost source of components for global auto manufacturers in the US market.

REVIVING US MANUFACTURING

Reviving American manufacturing and bringing back factory jobs has been a central element of Donald Trump's political identity since he announced his candidacy for the US presidency in 2016.

Past administrations created policies allowing American companies to move production to places like China and Mexico which Trump had vowed to bring back to the US. He had faced so much criticisms from the media and the Democrats however, the deal was completed with the trade war with China and the eye opening arrival of COVID-19.

TRUMP'S TRADE WAR WITH CHINA

President Trump like other leaders around the world have long accused China of unfair trading practices and intellectual property theft, but only Trump was bold and courageous to take on the Chinese single-handedly.

Before and after his election, China began to have the perception that America was trying to curb its rise as a global economic power.

Trump ran an anti-interventionist America First! Campaign,

"We will stop racing to topple foreign regimes that we know nothing about, that we shouldn't be involved with... instead, our focus must be on defeating terrorism and destroying ISIS, and we will."

Trump's rhetoric was similar to what he said during the election campaign when he railed against the war in Iraq.

"Leave the world to its troubles; the U.S. has infrastructure to build and a country to make great again."

His leadership focus was so detested by China, and was even more detested by the Democrats and the mainstream media.

The president's tariff policy aimed to encourage consumers to buy American products was intended to make imported goods more expensive.

After initial talks with China got nowhere, he threatened and eventually carried out his threat by imposing tariffs on more than

$360bn (£268bn) of Chinese goods, of which China retaliated with tariffs on more than $110bn of US products.

There were three more rounds of tariffs in 2018, and a fourth one in September 2019 followed from Washington, with the latest targeting Chinese imports, from meat to musical instruments, with a 15% duty.

China then retaliated, not only did China target American farmers with tariffs, trade allies like Canada and Mexico were also caught up in President Trump's move to tax imported steel triggered by

China as he fulfilled a 2016 campaign promise.

FARMERS THE GREAT US PATRIOTS

Also affected was the years-long negotiation over the US-Mexico-Canada (USMCA) Agreement, which created great uncertainty in the two big neighbouring markets.

President Trump has a great affection for America's farmers who were among the hardest hit in the year-long trade. Soybeans, the most valuable U.S. farm export, was at a 16-year low in 2018, since the trade war, and they were to benefit in the aid package from the US Department of Agriculture who were to pay the farmers according to geographic location rather than by crop.

Farmers have always been a key part of the Trump political base and the president took several steps to shore up the support of the agricultural industry,

"Farmers are great patriots, they understand that they're doing this for the country. And we'll make it up to them. And, in the end, they're going to be much stronger than they are right now."

For about a year, the Chinese tariffs wiped out what was once the US biggest foreign market for soya beans, which sent the prices plummeting and the farmers almost going out of business. As a result, the president paid out $28 billion in federal aid to help those hurt by his trade war with China which overturned an Obama-era rule despised by farmers.

Many farmers stuck by the president and fully supported him, believing that the new trade deals will make the pain from the tariffs worthwhile.

As such, the newly signed USMCA and preliminary, phase one China deal which provided some stability for markets gave farmers a sigh of relief.

Farmers in the cotton-growing Mississippi Delta states were the greatest beneficiaries of the program. Other beneficiaries were Illinois, the country's top soybean producer, and Iowa, the top corn- and hog-producing stat

President Trump had completed very tough negotiations with China around the end of 2019 and in early January 2020, Trump and China's Vice Premier Liu held a long-anticipated ceremony to sign a "Phase One" US-China trade deal, with China promising to buy billions of dollars more in agricultural products from US farmers and Trump imposed a 25% tariff on $250 bn. on most of China's goods into the US, most of which was to be given to the farmers in three payments totalling around $47 billion. by the year end 2020.

The agreement further stipulated that China will make purchases far in excess of what it bought in 2017, totaling $32 billion over the next two years.

Going into January 2020 – just as rumours about the coronavirus began fluttering out of China and China soon began to buckle under Trump's tariffs,

Chinese officials said tariffs on some goods would be cut to 5% from 10%, and on others from 5% to 2.5% and a partial resolution was agreed in January 2020, with China promising to boost imported US goods by $200bn.

This was in response to President Trump's "phase one" agreement. Under the so-called "phase one" deal signed in January 2020, China pledged to boost US imports by $200 billion above 2017 levels and strengthen intellectual property rules, and the US agreed to halve some of the new tariffs it had imposed on China.

The White House said it would tackle additional issues in a "phase two" deal and then came COVID-19, which exposed China to so much criticism and mistrust.

TRUMP ON GLOBALISATION

Globalisation was hailed as the ultimate in human progress, with the model based on loosening the controls on capital and the building of global supply chains. By the end of 2016, the model which impacted mainly the US and the UK-created recurrent financial crises and corrosive inequality and as soon as Trump came into office the flames of globalisation soon began to extinguish with China accusing the US of deliberately destroying the world order.

Millions of people had been lifted out of poverty, and most of these lived in China, the manufacturing hub of the world, with its cheap labour and cheaper manufacturing processes which made it very expensive to manufacture goods, from penny priced pencils to life saving medicines.

Across Asia, Europe and Africa, China's globalisation affected most parts of the world with their Road Initiative Infrastructure projects which had a dual purpose – to provide a market for Chinese goods and to extend Beijing's reach in parts of the world because America's power had been weakened.

Many countries were already pondering and worried about China's globalisation trend while the world sat on their laurels and watched as China strutted their might across the world all of which led to the annual anti-globalisation riots. Every three years the International Monetary Fund and the World Bank hold their annual meetings and since 2000, these meetings in Prague get besieged by anti-globalisation rioters, all of which stopped abruptly as soon as Trump took on globalisation single-handedly.

Trump was openly mocked by the Democrats and the media, if only they understood that having a business background meant the ability to execute macro-economics policies with calculated moves within a dynamic changing economy.

Trump's initial tactical move was to impose tariffs on China of which the democrats and the media laughed and claimed that the tariffs would be detrimental to the US because world power China was bound to retaliate with their own tariffs. As the rhetoric and tariffs escalated, it soon became clear that Trump didn't just want China to play fair. He wanted to sever the economic relationship completely.

"We are better off without them."

After which he ordered American companies to look for alternatives to China and consider bringing their companies back home or he would impose taxes on them. Many analysts had laughed off that threat.

"He can't do that", they said.

But he did. Unfortunately, globalization also came along with more unsavoury effects as poorer nations and groups of people got robbed of their natural resources, and blue-collar workers lost jobs due to outsourcing all the jobs to China.

In fact, China became the greatest pollutants as a result of their manufacturing, which rich people were already positioned to benefit immensely from, so it would be no surprise that George Soros and almost any entrepreneur and most world governments were in favour of globalization and yet, George Soros emerges as a major funder of 'Global Climate Strike' groups and this became more aggressive when Trump became president – they would protest wherever Trump was holding a meeting but cowardly ignored China at all counts.

Globalisation brought in the Climate Extremist sponsored by Billionaire Soros and other billionaire stakeholders in Climate change such as Pelosi who had funnelled funds into her husbands and son's failed 'wind' business, all of whom were fighting tooth and nails to protect their interests.

By the end of May 2020, Google severed business ties with Huawei following an executive order from President Trump blacklisting the company and requiring all American companies to seek government approval before dealing with the company after it was placed on an "entity list" by the US Commerce Department.

The UK's government has since drawn up plans to remove telecom equipment made by the Chinese manufacturer Huawei from the nation's 5G networks by 2023.

Another global trade issue related to the Chinese technology organisation Huawei. With absolute hindsight, despite more than a year of intense lobbying the world leaders, the Trump administration had accused Huawei of having ties to China's Communist Party, which posed a national security threat to not only the US but also to their allies. The British government stood their ground however, around the end of January 2020 announced it would allow the company to provide equipment in some portions of a next-generation network to be built in the coming years. The British decision was crucial in a broader fight for technology supremacy between the United States and China. Britain, a key American ally, was the most important country to reject the White House warnings that Huawei was an instrument of Beijing.

Britain's membership in the "five eyes" intelligence-sharing group of countries, which also includes Australia, Canada and New Zealand, gave the outcome an added significance – possibly for fear of being caught up between the United States and China in their tech-cold war. As a result, the US threatened to withhold intelligence for not banning Huawei, while Chinese representatives menacingly warned of economic retaliation.

The other world leaders soon yielded to his decision on Huawei because in early July 2020, the UK decided to follow Washington's lead on Huawei which marked a significant departure from Prime Minister Boris Johnson's previous stance.

The president soon had the last laugh with the arrival of COVID-19 which justified the reasons behind the president's manufacturing policies. As it happened, all the masks, test kits, medications, respirators and ventilators required to fight the virus were all being made in China, who were in turn, reluctant to release the PPE and when they did – they were either faulty or inadequate, which led to Trump having them all made in the US, this strategic move created more US jobs and helped the economy during the lockdown.

COVID-19 by its own hands provided the opportunity for the president to deliver his strategic war on globalism strategy.

Whether the pandemic which globally brought the world to its knees, begging for masks, gloves absolute social communistic society was an accident, or a deliberate convenient globalist pandemic to stop the president, by end of July 2020 it was becoming to seem like the hands of God to push through and justify President Trump's policies by exposing the threats to lives when the world realised that most of the arsenal needed to fight COVID-19 were in China, who were very reluctant to release the lifesaving PPE, the Democrats that never co-operated with the president to save lives but spent the duration of the pandemic blocking and obstructing all the initiatives to help the American people and of course the impact of the journalists that simply continued fanning and stoking hate and fear.

PROTECTOR OF THE UNBORN AND THE NEWLY BORN.

In 2003, then-Illinois State Senator Obama stated plainly that he believed abortions should be legal in all situations and even late in a pregnancy.

This stance left many medical staff faced with the gruesome horrific tasks of having live babies being injected to death – soon after being born alive.

Self-professed Roman Catholics Jo Biden and Nancy Pelosi opposed all legislations that would have given legal protection to infants who survived abortion attempts – including full term healthy babies.

Obama had no intention of 'reducing abortions' so during his 2008 campaign, he told Planned Parenthood Action that his first act in the White House would be to sign the Freedom of Choice Act—a bill that would codify the right to abortion by eliminating all federal and state-level restrictions on the procedure, which served to 'sweep away hundreds of anti-abortion laws and policies'.

Through its clinics, Planned Parenthood provides a variety of reproductive health services, such as birth control, abortion and sexually-transmitted disease testing at its clinics, online and in schools.

Over 51% of Planned Parenthood's clinic income comes from abortion. In addition to its $320 million in clinic income and $223 million in private donations from the likes of Soros and Microsoft's Bill Gates, Planned Parenthood receives $487.4 million a year from taxpayers.

The two main controversies about Planned Parenthood are their strategic locations. Most of their clinics are based in mainly black American neighbourhoods and the clinics are known for the dark shadowy gory activities of selling "foetal tissues" of the aborted babies mostly for research and other dark arts.

Trump as we know is very pro-life and as such his policies were going to impact Obama's macabre abortion policies.

Donald Trump asked Congress to pass legislation to ban what he called "late-term" abortions. He introduced a two-year-old girl, who survived despite being born at just 21 weeks and six days. The president said, "Ellie reminds us that every child is a miracle of life. Thanks to modern medical wonders, 50% of very premature babies delivered at the hospital where Ellie was born now survive....

"Our goal should be to ensure that every baby has the best chance to thrive and grow just like Ellie. That is why I am asking the Congress to provide an additional $50 million to fund neonatal research for America's youngest patients....

"That is also why I am calling upon the members of Congress here tonight to pass legislation finally banning the late-term abortion of babies."

The president added, "...whether we are Republican, Democrat, or Independent, surely we must all agree that every human life is a sacred gift from God!"

That last sentence was clearly a plea for babies' lives directed at Pelosi who claims to be a Catholic and is hopefully aware of the Catholic stance on abortion.

Trump did not stop there; he issued a proposal to cut federal funding for organisations that offer or mention abortion to their patients.

Planned Parenthood, insisted that the proposal was 'dangerous' and 'outrageous' and would 'have devastating consequences', while anti-abortion activists thanked President Trump for 'delivering on a key promise'.

Trump still had not finished. He took his policy on abortion worldwide, cutting off all funding to any overseas organisation or clinic that will not agree to a complete ban or even discussing it.

The founder of Planned Parenthood, the rabidly anti-Catholic Margaret Sanger, was a notorious racist and anti-Catholic bigot, but with the advent of the Black Lives Matter (BLM) movement, around June 2020, the abortion organisation decided to hide her past and started with removing Sanger's name from its buildings. In doing this, many have not realised that the clinics are targeted at black lives or may even forget why nearly 80% of their abortion facilities are located within walking distance of Black neighbourhoods in fairness to (BLM), I did not as well, until I started re-searching on this book.

President Trump had cut federal funding to Planned Parenthood. If they were principled, they would embrace natural law, but if they did, they would have to go out of business. Many now want Planned Parenthood's historic racism, and its monistic fixation on aborting black babies, to be taught in the schools in the bid to ensure that their despicable legacy is never erased.

Interestingly, they are being funded by you guessed it – the billionaire George Soros and Bill Gates.

The president is against late-term abortions, a key part of his State of the Union address in February 2020 when he criticized efforts in Virginia and New York that would allow women to terminate pregnancies after 24 weeks and killing babies after they were literally born alive at the digression of the mother.

The president affirmed religious liberty in his State of the Union address when he stated,

---

"In America, we don't punish prayer. We don't tear down crosses. We don't ban symbols of faith. We don't muzzle preachers and pastors. In America, we celebrate Faith, cherish religion, and raise our sights to the Glory of God."

His stance on abortion alone gained him the support of at least 75% of the US Catholics and Christians. During the Obama administration many felt uncomfortable wearing a crucifix at work or in public – this soon changed when Trump came into office and with that alone, many including myself; are praying for a second term in order to be able to comfortably wear a Crucifix for another 4 years.

The Democrats anti-Christian stances are so numerous and poignant; most absurd of all, Obama nominated three pro-abortion ambassadors to the Vatican, which had earned him the title 'America's Most Biblically Hostile President'. In contrast, the New York Times had reported in June 22, 2016 that, "the Republican nominee (Donald Trump) spoke with a group of conservative Christians and promised to appoint anti-abortion Supreme Court Justices and get department store employees to say "Merry Christmas."

Also, California Attorney General Kamala Harris received over $80,000 in donations after using her power of office to go after a journalist, Robert Daleiden that exposed how Planned Parenthood were trafficking black baby body parts not only that, most inhumane of all was that even full term babies that survived failed abortions – here I literally mean born alive, were refused medical treatment and she voted to have them killed by injections.

In 2016, 81% of evangelicals had voted for President Trump, this number is soon to increase with the Catholic support as a result of his anti-abortion stance. Apart from the fact that his wife Melania Trump was born and raised a Catholic, the President has stated on numerous occasions, that he is pro-life and he has since gained the title, 'Protector of the Unborn and the Newly Born'.

HEALTH CARE INSURANCE

I found the US health care and insurance ever so complicated during my research and requested idiot level explanations, even from several of my friends and family that live in the US, and they could not come up with the explanation. Quite unlike our National Health Service (NHS), the most enviable single-payer healthcare system in the world, the US healthcare system is rather complicated, but I have managed to make some sense of it all.

Unlike the American system, our healthcare system is primarily funded by the government from general taxation, plus a small amount from National Insurance contributions that we pay from our salaries. The NHS provides free healthcare to all legal UK residents – however, we all have the option of paying for private health care insurance. This has the benefit of providing you with 5-star hotel service albeit in a hospital. Wider hospital beds, fruits and flowers, bottled drinking water, 5-star gourmet food, massages, power shower bathrooms, 50-inch television, but most important of all, the chance to jump the national health waiting list by up to 90%.

Quite simply, Medicaid is the United States program that helps with medical costs for people with limited income and resources. Medicaid also offers benefits not normally covered by the standard medical insurance, including nursing home care and personal care services. You qualify for Medicaid, if the company you work for does not provide employment-based health care benefit perks, you are unemployed or you are over 65 years old. The Americans also have a second option, Obamacare, a paid medical insurance which the majority of Americans who did not qualify for Medicaid had to have.

Obama had his plan renamed Obama-care – the Patient Protection and Affordable Care Act 2010 (ACA). The primary goal was to slow the rising burden of health care on the state by taking steps to make health insurance more available and more affordable to those who needed it the most. The act also required everyone to carry health insurance or pay a 'tax penalty'.

Also, it ensured that people got employment-based health insurance as a benefit from their employer whereby the company would pay part of the monthly cost, known as a premium – and the company was fined if the company did not comply.

But many Americans could not afford to have Obama-care, and simply took their chances of not falling ill. This was because they were either denied coverage by the insurance company, were charged a higher premium, or simply because their condition could not be treated.

Some had a chronic illness, called a 'pre-existing condition', and the insurance companies wouldn't even offer them coverage. If many of these people needed to go into hospital, they often just didn't pay the bill, leaving the hospital to claim the cost from the emergency Medicaid plan, which simply raised the cost of health-care for everyone because it was re-charged to the federal health budget

Another problem with Obama-care was that 3-5 million people lost their employment-based health insurance because many businesses did not find it practical to run and it was more cost-effective to pay the penalty and as such, many employees had to rely on Medicaid which put worse strain on the federal cost for health care.

Further problems with Obama-care was that it contained more obstacles for 4 main groups of people;

- High earners
- Those who had been healthy and had paid low rates in the past
- Larger firms that didn't insure their employees before the law but had to shell out for their employees over night

In a nutshell, although Obama-care was supposed to provide access to medical care, while insurance coverage had increased, health care costs became expensive, particularly for the young. The most energetic new workers had to pay very high costs of insurance, and those on higher salaries had to pay higher tax to cover for their health care insurance, forcing many to go without. In fact, people preferred to pay the fine rather than the insurance. Quite simply, you either paid for very expensive health insurance or paid a fine for non-compliance.

The very day after President Trump was sworn in on 21st January 2017, he signed an executive order instructing administration officials 'to waive, defer, grant exemptions from, or delay' implementing parts of the Affordable Care Act.

This was to reduce the complicated Obama-care system and give the American people a choice that will best suit them without the fines.

Trump reduced the penalty for not having insurance to exactly $0.00. Just like the UK system.

President Trump also promised and did lower prescription drug costs and to repeal Obama-care.

Although he hasn't been successful in repealing the Affordable Care Act completely, he had weakened it considerably by June 2020.

The president wanted all to get cheaper medication. He suggested that drug-makers disclose their prices in advertising which enabled people to shop for the best value medication.

Another campaign promise was to allow the American citizens to purchase drugs overseas – but we all know what he thinks of buying from foreign phar-maceuticals – his preference is to 'buy American' and the advent of COVID-19 has resulted in this being the best route as most pharmaceuticals have relocated back to the United States.

Trump decided to build on Telehealth expansions that he had promised which became very relevant during the pandemic to more than double the number of allowable telehealth services. In August 2020 he commented that,

> "We worked with the leaders of major health insurance companies to ensure coverage for the telehealth visits related to Coronavirus. We cut red tape to allow many services to be conducted by phone, rather than video, which is much simpler, providing a much easier option for many seniors in particular.
>
> "We allocated nearly $165 million through the CARES Act to support nearly 1,800 small rural hospitals who have done an incredible job, as well as $11.5 million to expand technical assistance for rural and underserved areas."

THE NATIONAL RIFLE ASSOCIATION OF AMERICA (NRA)

The National Rifle Association of America (NRA) is a gun rights advocacy group founded to advance rifle marksmanship and to teach firearm safety and they have almost 5 million members.

President Trump has always focussed on fixing defective gun legislation already in place to avoid infringing the Second Amendment rights of Americans – Right to Bear Arms.

In May 2016, Trump received an endorsement from the NRA and he has repeatedly assured the members that he will protect their rights and will prevent any legislation that impedes their right to bear arms. Trump asserted that, "an overwhelming majority of people who go through background checks are law-abiding gun owners...too many states fail to properly put criminal and mental-health records into the database system."

In January 2020, when the media reported a most alarming scare pro-gun rally at Virginia capital, where thousands of armed protesters turned out for what was called a 'Trump-supported' gun rally.

Many sat glued to the television as the mainstream media provided their commentary on the day's event.

On the day of the event, we sat glued to the television and watched over

15,000 gun rights advocates converging at the town of Richmond to protest the Democrats proposed gun control laws that prohibited the sale of the popular AR-15 style rifles assault weapons bill. Most of the protesters were armed and showed off their rifles and were in tactical gear and displayed their homemade posters.

Much to the disappointment of the media, the rally ended peacefully despite excitement and confidence from the mainstream media and democrats that there was bound to be an incident.

This peaceful protest confirmed Trump's views on gun controls,

---

"What we need to do is fix the system we have and make it work as intended. What we don't need to do is expand a broken system."

COVID-19 brought on the 'lock down' measures. This led to huge queues as Americans 'panic-bought' toilet papers and guns amid the virus outbreak. Many reportedly said they were preparing for a breakdown in public order over COVID-19.

As the queues formed in front and around gun stores, the anti-gun activists criticised them on all the main media news networks and parroted 4 main reasons why people should think twice before purchasing the guns;

- A gun is more likely to be stolen than used in self-defence.
- Unsecured guns in the home create risks of unintentional shootings by children.
- Guns are the most lethal means of suicide attempts.
- Guns in the home increase risks to victims of domestic and family violence.

The sale of guns soon levelled off and even began falling however, when it was announced that more than 16,000 prisoners were to be granted early releases due to concerns about the spread of coronavirus inside jailhouses – many pro-gun owners held on tightly to their guns, a week later, news broke that some released inmates were committing new crimes – the queues grew longer with new registrations for guns. The queues and sale of guns increased even more when thousands of protesters across the country gathered to demand justice for George Floyd, Breonna Taylor, and other black people killed by the police, with their rallying cry to defund the police.

Defunding the police does not necessarily mean getting rid of the police altogether. Rather, it would mean reducing police budgets and ridiculously reallocating the funds education, public health, and housing and youth services. The twisted reasons for defunding did not make sense and increased the sale of baseball bats and made the queues around gun stores even longer in preparation for self-defense.

"To the people who fly private but lecture us about the environment. To the people who live in gated communities but lecture us about building walls. To the people who travel with armed guards and lecture us about guns, your bottomless hypocrisy is why America choses Trump." – Candace Owens

FIRESTORM ON THE 2015 PARIS AGREEMENT ON CLIMATE

President Trump holds a rather moderate view on climate change and refers to climate activists as 'prophets of doom' whereas the Democrats, climate change activists, mainstream media and celebrities would make climate change their weapon against him.

The climate change activists, sponsored by George Soros, Microsoft's Bill Gates and media mogul Bloomberg claim that increased heat, spontaneous wildfires, and drought and insect outbreaks are all linked to climate change.

President Trump did not help their cause when he withdrew from the Paris treaty set up by former President Obama.

The Paris Agreement sets out a global framework to avoid dangerous climate change by limiting global warming to well below 2°C with efforts to limit it to 1.5°C. It also aimed to strengthen countries' ability to deal with the impacts of climate change and support them in their efforts. The big issue here is that many people are not fully convinced of their exaggerated purpose.

President Trump has strongly criticized the 2015 Paris Agreement on climate reached by President Barack Obama's administration, arguing that;

- China – the manufacturing hub of the world had been left to flourish, since the climate activists only targeted weaker countries who were all susceptible to accusations of 'political correctness'. In effect, as soon as they stepped foot into China to protest, he would back them 100%.
- The president's second and most important criticism was that he did not like the idea of the US being the largest donor. President Obama committed the United States to contributing US$3 billion to the Green Climate Fund and the Fund set itself a goal of raising $100 billion a year by 2020, and none of the other countries' contributions, when totaled up, could not match the US.

When researching volcanoes, I found several studies that stated that the eruption of a volcano, the greatest impact on climate change can cause a cooling or warming effect on the Earth's surface. The cooling effect can last for months to years depending on the characteristics of the eruption.

The papers all confirmed that volcanoes have also caused global warming over millions of years during times in Earth's history when extreme amounts of volcanism occurred, releasing greenhouse gases into the atmosphere, and contributing to warming of the atmosphere.

Other lesser causes of global warming, in order of the magnitude of their impact, are mainly from:

- Fossil Fuel – a general term for buried deposits of organic materials, formed from decayed plants and animals that have been converted to crude oil, coal, natural gas, or heavy oils by exposure to heat and pressure in the earth's crust over hundreds of millions of years
- Methane from cattle and rice paddies
- Nitrogen Oxides from farming

While there is some evidence that climate change occurs because of human intervention such as pollution, there are other studies that dispute this claim.

Recently, scientists have confirmed that Greenland's ice is melting four times faster than thought—what it means is that Greenland may be approaching a dangerous tipping point, with implications for global sea-level rise.

What they did not mention was that active volcanic eruptions discovered beneath Antarctic ice sheets could be contributing to rapidly melting glaciers which may be adding to climate change and may have induced the sea level to rise. Scientists have warned that this hidden source of heat must be taken into consideration when predicting future sea level rise.

Quite as recent as 2014, some predicted that it would be the hottest year that we have ever had, but the fact of the matter is, it ended up not so.

They had projected that in 2010 there would be a rise in the ocean by about 20 foot. So far, into 2020, the sea levels are still pretty normal and staying about where they should be.

According to many reports, only about 1% of all scientists believe that there is a problem with the temperature on the earth. In support of the climate activists, I found out information about the river Thames freezing up in January 1963, which was the coldest January since 1814, the last time the Thames had frozen. In 1963, the experts had heralded a mini ice age but this ended within three months.

President Trump is very smart about the long-term ramifications to the 2015 Paris 'treaty'. Like many, he has stated that if the easily influenced industrialized nations commit themselves to this agreement, they will leave their manufacturing base hostage to ridiculous burdensome regulations and agreements – from China mostly and as such, Trump removed the US from the 2015 Paris Treaty.

In late January 2020, 'anti-climate billionaires' and the world's leading politicians and business people converged at the deep snow of Davos after having spent their time at the World Economic Forum (WEF), talking about the climate crisis. Also in attendance were the climate change supporters on 'How to stop Republican front-runner Donald Trump', most of whom had attended in their private jets to the shock of both climate change activists and dissenters.

The meeting included Apple's Tim Cook, Google's Larry Page, Napster creator and Facebook investor Sean Parker, and Tesla Motors and Space-X magnate Elon Musk. The point here is that they all flew in for the meeting, and worse, in their private jets – which sent the message that there are moderates naturally concerned like the president and many others. Quite unlike the fanatical pretentions activists and celebrities and even Obama the progenitor of the 2015 Paris Agreement; when in August 2019, he revealed to the world that he had splashed out on a $15 million home just by the sea side – disputing all claims made by the activists that in 12 years must of the seaside will be submerged and all should fear for cities and coasts around the world.

President Trump withdrew the US from the Paris climate agreement in 2019 which the billionaire advocates and sponsors agreed to make up the shortfall of $100 billion per annum – not from their purses but from the ordinary US taxpayers.

Even Harrison Ford was caught taking his son to school in one of his 10 planes, an $18 million private jet soon after delivering a speech at the UN Climate Action Summit.

It is worth noting that various Hollywood celebrities and billionaires are ramping up efforts to drive the clean energy advances needed to meet the goals of the accord and put the brakes on dangerous climate change—with or without the Trump administration and thankfully without the American taxpayers' $100 billion dollar contribution. And then came COVID-19 and global economic crash. President Donald Trump's World Economic Forum Davos address in January 2020; "In rebuilding America, we are also fully committed to developing our workforce. We are lifting people from dependence to independence – because we know the single best anti-poverty program is a pay check. To be successful, it is not enough to invest in our economy – we must invest in our people."

Almost with ingenious foresight- the US had pulled out on time, being the only country funding the scheme. The air and the environment during the lockdown was well into the expected levels and it will be interesting to see how this pans out with the other nations in the future months now that their countries are trying to rebuild their respective economies and when manufacturing commences in their respective countries and no more in China.

GREEN NEW DEAL

Another controversial subject is the president's stance on the Green New Deal (GND), the United States legislation that aims to address climate change. This aims to achieve an overall balance between emissions of carbon produced and emissions taken out of the atmosphere in order to attain – Net zero, the removal of as much carbon in the atmosphere as is put into it.

Biden wants to spend $1.7 trillion on addressing climate change, and his deadline for net zero is 2050.

The key problem here is that the president sees it as an utter fantasy and said that the deal would 'kill millions of jobs' and cost not just $1.7 trillion, but hundreds of trillions of dollars according to the projections presented by the Democrats and various other conservative groups. The Green New Deal resolution doesn't mention how the US government, which has $22 trillion of debt, would pay for it.

President Trump did reject the mainstream climate euphoria but has led on issues related to the environment;

- The US currently gets 80% of its energy from coal, petroleum, and natural gas. Hence, the kind of overhaul the deal is calling for would be very expensive and require significant government intervention and gradual decline over the years but not as the sudden drastic closures as demanded by the Democrats.
- Many people have seen bird cemeteries under wind turbines here in the UK and no one has cared to address the threat of wind turbines to wildlife.
- The Environmental Protection Agency (EPA) confirmed that there have been major air quality improvements in the past decades as a result of the Clean Air Act and Clean Water Act, in the past couple of years.
- The Clean Air Act requires the Environmental Protection Agency to develop and enforce regulations to protect the public from airborne contaminants known to be hazardous to human health.
- The Clean Water Act is the primary federal law in the United States governing water pollution. Its objective is to restore and maintain the chemical, physical, and biological integrity of the nation's waters; recognizing the responsibilities of the states in addressing pollution and providing assistance to states to do so, including funding for publicly owned treatment works for the improvement of wastewater treatment; and maintaining the integrity of wetlands.

An interesting point here is that the worst offenders are the Chinese and several green organisations in China, of which Speaker Pelosi's husband and several other democrats are on the board.

Pelosi's husband invested in solar firm SunEdison's expansion before a 2014 stock rally and company expansion – obviously through insider information.

Pelosi's office did not respond to questions about the timing of the purchase and whether she or her husband had any advance knowledge of the deal.

As fate would have it, the greed led to SunEdison expanding too fast – and even $1.5 billion in subsidies and loan guarantees did not save the "clean" energy company from bankruptcy.

Several economists have suggested that the federal government adopt a 'revenue-neutral carbon tax' to decrease emissions without exacerbating the fiscal imbalance; whereby the tax would be paid by businesses and industries that produce carbon dioxide through their operations.

The tax will reduce the output of greenhouse gases and carbon dioxide into the atmosphere and all tax collected by the government are returned to the households and businesses through some mechanism, like tax cuts.

The coronavirus pandemic affected nearly every aspect of life in the world, and solar and wind power was no exception. Again, almost with prophetic foresight by the president or the hand of God, in the attempt to contain the virus, the factories that make solar panels and wind turbines which are all in China were all shut down, and not by Trump – which ironically slowed the production of green energy equipment and subsequently carbon emissions.

In early August, this great president signed the Great American Outdoors Bipartisan law that marked the largest-ever investment into America's national parks and public lands. It will also create more than 100,000 infrastructure-related jobs, much needed after the COVID-19 lock down.

REPRIEVE AND FREEDOM FOR PRISONERS

THE FIRST STEP ACT OF 2018

The First Step Act of 2018 is one of the biggest legislative victories for advocates of criminal justice reform in years which directly impacted many black inmates and their families. The aim of this law signed by President Trump did not only release prisoners but also prepared individuals to re-enter their communities as responsible citizens by allowing them to serve a chunk of their sentences out of prisons in home confinement and equipping them with support structures as they transitioned out of custody.

Not all celebrities have been against Trump. Most give their full support in words but those that acted in deeds as well as in words include notably Kim Kardashian. In 2018, Kardashian West lobbied the White House on behalf of a grandmother jailed for life, Ms Johnson was given a life sentence for a non-violent drugs conviction in 1996, and became a symbol for many of harsh sentencing. The person responsible was the City Attorney of San Francisco Kamala Harris who had criminalised and put thousands of black Americans in jail simply for smoking marijuana.

Kim Kardashian West visited the White House in 2019 with three women that were recently freed from prison to thank the President. They had been jailed for drug-related and white-collar crimes, and all had young children when imprisoned. President Trump had cut short the jail sentences of Crystal Munoz, Judith Negron and Tynice Hall, typically, this was not reported in the news.

In July 2019, with incredible foresight, Trump released over 3,000 people from prison, many of them were black African Americans and most of those released had earned good time for non-violent offences. Being released under the First Step Act enabled former inmates to settle into normal home life and many had been serving lengthy prison terms after federal prosecutors such as Kamala Harris had convicted them of non-violent offenses.

Another lady serving a life sentence for a drug conviction was released after serving twenty years. These were typical of the harsh sentences meted out by the Obama administration.

Releasing prisoners was a positive and direct impact on the rise of the black Trump base.

In February 2020, President Trump granted clemency to eleven people in total, including former Illinois governor Rod Blagojevich. Many had fallen foul of the harshest sentences in the previous administration and had appealed to President Barack Obama for their sentences to be commuted before he left office, but the requests were denied.

With leadership and foresight, the coronavirus pandemic also led to the release of even more prisoners – this particular strategic undertaking was easy to implement because the process was already in place.

HEALTH BILL

Back in October 2019, the president had signed a health bill which raised the legal smoking age from 18 to 21 for cigarettes, however, FLOTUS launched the Truth Initiative which was about the damage that even vaping does to the lungs. Little did we know that the coronavirus that was to sweep the world would be a contagious respiratory illness caused by viruses that infect the lungs directly?

The aim of the Truth Initiative was to crack down on youth smoking which damaged their underdeveloped lungs that would have increased the death rates – although the expert have stated that few people under 65 died for the pandemic, those with respiratory were said to be affected by the virus and as such, FLOTUS may have saved thousands of lives from awareness of her initiative.

NOBEL PEACE PRIZE – PRESIDENT TRUMP A MAN OF PEACE

NORTH KOREA

After decades of mutual hostility, North Korean leader Kim Jong-un and US President Donald Trump met in person in May 2017.

No sitting US president has ever met a North Korean leader, but there were repeated attempts to talk in order to get North Korea to denuclearize.

North Korea had been isolated for decades because of its well-documented human rights abuses and its pursuit of nuclear weapons, in defiance of international laws. The last major effort – the Six Party talks – had collapsed in 2008, largely because North Korea refused to allow inspectors to verify that it had shut down its nuclear programme.

Several bids to restart the talks had collapsed, including the 2012 talks when North Korea launched another rocket, two weeks after announcing a "leap day"

(29 February) agreement with the US that had promised food aid in return for inspections and a moratorium on missile tests.

Trump has long been bothered by North Korean Leader Kim Jong Un's threats against the United States. They had also continued to carry out nuclear tests, and had boasted that they now had missiles that could reach the US. President Trump's response was, "North Korea best not make any more threats to the United States, they will be met with fire and fury like the world has never seen ... he has been very threatening beyond a normal state. They will be met with fire, fury and frankly power the likes of which this world has never seen before."

Following behind the scenes negotiations, President Trump and Kim Jong-un decided to meet, to pledge peace and security at the Singapore summit.

Several days before the meeting, the negative press did not think it possible since no other president had ever achieved that level of peace agreement, and Trump was the last person to attempt that, let alone do it.

The various commentators stated that it would end up an embarrassing attempt for Trump.

But in May 2018, Trump and North Korea's Kim Jong-un met face to face for the 'milestone' meeting.

After their nearly five-hour summit, the US president promised 'security guarantees' to Pyongyang and announced that war games with South Korea would cease. What however did not cease for at least two weeks after the meeting were the viral memes showing former President Obama peeping into North Korea.

This meeting had earmarked President Trump for the Nobel Peace Prize. The presentation would have to be delayed until the 2020 elections because tempers were rising and being presented with the award before the elections would only serve to give the president an unfair advantage at the polls.

Both talks and negotiations were later to be grudgingly recognised by the mainstream media. Being Trump, as far as peace was concerned, he did not stop at North Korea – included in his world peace initiative was the Trump peace plan, 'the Deal of the Century', this was predicted to end the conflict between Israelis and Palestinians and clear all claims made by both parties to the conflict.

President Trump was also responsible for brokering peace between Ethiopia and Eritrea, using his influence in the peace talks which also included the United Arab Emirates and Saudi Arabia.

MIDDLE EAST

Before President Trump took office, Iran was imposing a serious threat to the Middle East regions and subsequently the whole world because they were increasing their nuclear capabilities.

The way that Obama thought around this was to set up an Iran nuclear deal with the Iranians. The agreement which was reached in 2015 between the Islamic Republic of Iran and a group of world powers; the United States, the United Kingdom, Russia, France, China and Germany.

The purpose of the deal was to limit Iran's nuclear program to being small, safe, and peaceful — and to impose invasive inspections to make sure Iran kept its end of the deal and remained exclusively peaceful.

In exchange, the Iran nuclear deal, formally known as the Joint Comprehensive Plan of Action, involved offering billions of American dollars in exchange, for no less than $700 million each month, to a grand total of around $11.9 billion, most of which ended in the pockets of several senior US and Iranian politicians.

The former administration had confirmed that Iran was a difficult one to fight so in order to maintain some peace and quiet in the world, Susan Rice went further to pay the terrorists ISEL headed by the Iranian general Abu Solemani – $400 million in exchange for four political hostages.

Like many, the Iranians had gambled on the Democrats winning the 2016 presidential elections – and then came Trump.

The Obama deal was disliked globally, but many leaders were frightened to do much about it; some chose to diplomatically stay quiet while others mouthed off on the media against Trump. To add more salt to injury, Trump went even further, he wanted a 'new' nuclear deal with Iran – sanctions – which he expressed in the 2019 G20 conference with world leaders.

Saudi Arabia backed Trump's decision to withdraw from Obama's Iran deal, and backed his plan to reinstate sanctions on the regime. Many claimed that Trump had broken the unilateral deal and that would most likely result in attacks unleashed on the world.

General Abu Solemani, the real enemy of the United States was at the centre of most, if not all terrorist attacks around the world that continued even after

Obama's deal was struck. He had targeted most of the attacks at the Americans and most of the terrorist attacks all over the world were linked to Iran's ISEL.

Also, the Iranians continued in their production of uranium, which they claimed was for domestic consumption.

In his efforts to make the Iranians to negotiate peace and to stop the build-up of their nuclear weapons, Trump would not pay out American dollars which he stated were much needed to help the people in the United States, and when they would not negotiate, he opted to apply sanction squeezes on the Iranians – which included an embargo on dealings with the country by the US, and a ban on selling aircraft and repair parts to Iranian aviation companies.

The sanctions were designed to pressure Iran to negotiate, but Iran's fiery response was to shoot down an unmanned US surveillance drone to which Trump announced that he was 'locked and loaded' for a retaliatory strike on Iran but on the day, the president abruptly aborted the attack.

Instead of wanting to know why, the media were on cue to promote the Democrats' hate campaigns – the media called him all sorts for not following up on his threat.

A few days later, in a press conference, the president stated that he was 'a man of peace' and may have to do business with the Iranians in the future – most important of all, the attack meant having untold millions of women and children as collateral damage and in the Christmas season which was against his most basic Christian conscience. The Democrats and the media did not see that as a reasonable excuse – they wanted Iranian women and children's blood.

In typical Trump style – he left them to stew. He was done – and continued with the harsher biting sanctions and focused on rumours about an outbreak of a 'flu like' virus at Wuhan in China.

Then, on January 1st 2020, a 200-strong group of hostile Iranians were heading towards the American embassy in Baghdad, headed by the general Abu Solemani and were preparing to attack the embassy.

This was reminiscent of the 2012 Benghazi attack when a coordinated attack against the United States consulate in Benghazi, Libya was carried out by members of the Islamic militant group led by one Ahmed Abu Khattala, who was under the direct command of the same Iranian general Abu Solemani.

On that occasion, the Americans under attack in the US diplomatic compound had immediately called on Obama and Hilary Clinton and pleaded for help.

While Obama and Hilary dithered, on the percentage of funds to extort for themselves on that crisis – several Americans, including the US Ambassador were mercilessly butchered.

Their murders, filmed and broadcast around the world, captured their bodies being dragged along the streets of Benghazi. In response to the murders, Joe Biden, Clinton, Obama and Susan Rice decided to send over $400 million in a cargo load of cash to the master commander to reduce the harassment of Americans around his Islamic territories around the world, meanwhile lying and hiding the truth from the American citizens that the attack was because of a video that was released in Libya – it was not. It was a terrorist attack. Hilary Clinton's lie to the Americans was to prevent the need for retaliation and as such condoning the desecration of the bodies of murdered Americans.

Back to January 2020 – The media was rife with Pelosi and the Democrat's impending impeachment of Trump, so the Iranian militant group had gambled on the distraction of the Trump administration from the 'hoax impeachment', and fired an apparent rocket which exploded in the high-security Green Zone within the US compound.

Trump was told that it would take at least three days to arrange the protocols, logistics and men to assist the soldiers at the American compound. In typical Trump style –

Trump sent reinforcement was at the American green zone compound within three hours of the intelligence getting to the president, by air from the Saudi Arabian base and the terrorist immediately dispersed and full re-enforcement from the United States arrived by air in the next six hours. Whilst the US aircraft carrier and a bomber taskforce began lurking towards Iraq on the Iranian waters. The US Army commando unit sent to the Naval Air Station Sigonella in Sicily, did not even deploy to Benghazi until after the attack was over.

This was the period that the group 'Democrats for Trump' was set up – his support base soared – not a US life was lost. The president was not done yet, he had ordered an unmanned drone to liquidate the general Abu Solemani without the transfer of a single US cent.

Hoping to dampen the decisive action taken by the president, the hateful

Democrats and their media sycophants continuously aired failed 2020 presidential candidate Warren who had called the mission 'a reckless' attack.

The BBC went on to proclaim Abu Solemani a revered figure and that Trump had acted merely to advance his interest – all negative reports soon ceased when social media countered their anti-Trump broadcasts with reminders and the ghosts of Benghazi – to the Democrats' and media disappointment, the people gradually remembered Benghazi, and that line of democratic attack abruptly disappeared from the media.

Scheming has been the core strategy of both the Democrats and the mainstream media, (lame stream media as renamed by President Trump). They did not have a single policy in place, except failed plots after failed plots, fuelled on by the mainstream media all of which gets implemented in the end. It was not surprising that when he decided to take down Iran General Soleimani, with foresight he did it without liaising with the Democrats and definitely not the media – the briefing to both houses came several days after the event.

Speaker Nancy Pelosi was angry because they were not given the chance to leak the 1st of January 2020 Iraq mission and went on to state that, "...the Soleimani killing does not make the country safer."

The general was taken out in Iraq which placed him supervising the failed attack at the US compound. General Soleimani had organised and had wreaked havoc on Christians in Iraq, Iran, Syria, and Lebanon for decades especially during Obama's administration. We all know what happened at Benghazi, when pallets of cash were sent to the terrorists during rather than help the Americans that were under siege.

Past presidents would have notified the so-called gang of eight small numbers of senior members of both the House and Senate in advance, before taking military action against a foreign power. The Democrats would have had a field day leaking the mission to the media and even to the general himself just to score political points.

The Iranians were still relying on CNN broadcasts that was beamed into their country and mustered up some courage, to hold anti Trump protests as they as the body of Abu Solemani was flown back to Iran for the funeral, this soon quelled overnight following the coronavirus visitations at Iran, many were dying, including several senior politician and in fact 8% of the Iranian parliament that had been ranting against Trump were infected.

Back in the US, the questions on social media were – what next will the Democrats come up with to derail the President's administration because the November elections were ten months away.

When President Trump announced concerns about the virus, still trying to save face from Trump's resurrection of the Benghazi ghost thrashing, the democrats termed his concerns as a deflection strategy from their looming impeachment of 5th of February.

There have been other peace initiatives globally that have been made.

In October 2017, Congress enacted and President Donald Trump signed the Women, Peace and Security Act of 2017 on a bipartisan basis. The law reflected a growing awareness that the wide-spread exclusion of women from peace processes and post-conflict governance, as well as the failure to protect and assist displaced women have been a key factor in the proliferation of wars and refugee crises globally, crises that impact America's own national security. The law protects and assists women threatened by violence and abuse from conflict and displacement, supports women's rights activists and movements abroad in his national security strategies – this was not reported in the media.

The negative attacks from the Democrats and the media have made the imminent award from the Norwegian Nobel Committee delayed.

However, the global leadership and decisive actions by President Trump during the war with the invisible enemy COVID-19 may well clench it sooner than we all expect.

It was then announced on 13 August 2020 that President Trump had secured a historic deal between Israel and the United Arab Emirates to advance peace and prosperity in the region – and pledged to take several steps to strengthen diplomatic relations, including exchanging embassies and ambassadors – the result of several negotiations brokered by Trump – if that does not secure the Nobel peace Prize, that would be absolutely laughable because the needs to bring back credibility rendering it meaningless and insignificant by awarding it to Obama only eleven days in office and my research could not find the peace he may have brokered in his entire eleven years in Office.

IN August 2020, President Donald J. Trump hosted the official signing ceremony for the historic peace agreements between Israel and Arab nations and this was not reported on in the UK. The President secured an agreement to normalize relations between the U.A.E. and Israel – the first such agreement between Israel and a major Arab country since 1994.

The peace deal has reached the nations across the Middle East and Africa who are now working together to build a more peaceful and prosperous future in the region.

EXECUTIVE ORDERS

In their attempts to be angry at me, several of my friends and family asked me to name anything that the president had done for the Americans during the pandemic – in my simple reply, I asked what about his Executive orders. Several replied that that was typical and that the president was known for ordering people about. Reader, here is what I could never explain to them. These are the president's primary tools for the management and mobilization of the vast resources of the federal government. Executive orders are controversial because they bypass approval from Congress, allowing the president to act on his own, in effect, it is bypassing Congress mainly because of their usual delays and obstructions. The Democrats would rather leave the people suffering instead of cooperating with the president during the desperate months of COVID-19. Some of the president's Executive orders included;

- Executive order implemented to protect police officers
- Executive order to target drug cartels
- Executive order for religious freedom
- Fighting the spread of COVID-19 by providing assistance to renters and homeowners
- Combating public health emergencies and strengthening national security by ensuring essential medicines, medical countermeasures, and critical inputs are made in the United States
- Addressing the threat posed by WeChat, and taking additional steps to address the national emergency with respect to the information and communications technology and services supply chain

- Addressing the threat posed by TikTok, and taking additional steps to address the national emergency with respect to the information and communications technology and services supply chain
- Improving rural health and telehealth access
- Aligning federal contracting and hiring practices with the interests of American workers
- Lowering prices for patients by eliminating kickbacks to middlemen
- Increasing drug importation to lower prices for American patients
- Access to affordable life-saving medications
- White House Hispanic Prosperity Initiative
- Building and rebuilding monuments to American heroes
- Protecting American monuments, memorials, and statues and combating recent criminal violence
- Strengthening the child welfare system for America's children
- Safe policing for safe communities
- Accelerating the nation's economic recovery from the COVID-19 emergency by expediting infrastructure investments and other activities
- Advancing international religious freedom
- Preventing online censorship
- Regulatory relief to support economic recovery
- Establishment of the Forced Labour Enforcement Task Force under Section 741 of the United States-Mexico-Canada Agreement Implementation Act
- Promoting American seafood competitiveness and economic growth
- Ordering the selected reserve of the armed forces to active duty
- Establishment of the Interagency Labor Committee for monitoring and enforcement Under Section 711 of the United States-Mexico-Canada Agreement Implementation Act
- Delegating Authority Under the Defense Production Act with respect to food supply chain resources during the national emergency caused by the outbreak of COVID-19
- Preventing hoarding of health and medical resources to respond to the spread of COVID-19
- Prioritizing and allocating health and medical resources to respond to the spread of COVID-19

- Establishment of the Interagency Committee on Trade in Automotive Goods Under Section 202A of the United States Mexico Canada Agreement Implementation Act
- Establishment of the Interagency Environment Committee for Monitoring and Enforcement under Section 811 of the United States-Mexico-Canada Agreement Implementation Act
- Reviving the National Space Council
- Combating human trafficking and online child exploitation in the United States
- Imposing sanctions with respect to additional sectors of Iran

SOME OF THE PRESIDENT'S ACCOMPLISHMENTS

"What magic wand does Trump have to bring back jobs to America" Obama, 2016.

We all now know that Trump did bring manufacturing and jobs back from mainland China.

The president has been in office for only three years and some of the Trump agenda is standard for a Republican president, but here are some of the achievements that I have managed to collate;

- Delayed students paying back student loans to the end of the year
- Payroll tax freeze for those earning less than $100,000
- Fighting the Spread of COVID-19 by providing assistance to renters and homeowners – directly targeting racial and ethnic minority groups at greater risk of eviction and homelessness or sharing of housing.
- White-collar criminal prosecutions have hit a 33-year low.
- The Justice Department defends state laws that remove many of the voting rolls.
- Addressing the threat posed by TikTok in terms of national security.
- Aligning federal contracting and hiring practices with the interests of American workers
- Lowering prices for patients by eliminating kickbacks to middlemen

- Military spending is on track at the same levels as during the height of the Iraq War.
- Installation more conservative judges and at an unprecedented pace.
- Reduced illegal immigration and drastic changes to immigration policy that go far beyond wall construction.
- Trump's goal of boosting America's natural resource extraction industries has been largely successful.
- Employment in coal mining has stabilized and is rising slightly in a reversal of recent trends.
- American oil output has soared to the point where net imports of crude oil and petroleum products are at their lowest level in generations and the country is likely to become a net exporter in the near future.
- Natural gas output, meanwhile, has soared to record highs.
- Huge the tax cuts which are expected to pay for themselves through faster economic growth.
- Sanctioned iron over missile program
- Responded to Syria with bombing
- Created task force to reduce crime
- Created commission on opioid addiction
- Combatting human trafficking
- Food stamp use lowest in seven years
- Reduced White House payroll
- Donating presidential salary
- Successful trip to North Korea
- Signed trade deal with China
- Designated North Korea a terrorist state
- ISIS lost virtually all of its territories
- Jerusalem as Israel's capital
- Trump recently signed three bills to benefit Native people. One gives compensation to the Spokane tribe for loss of their lands in the mid-1900s, one funds Native language programs, and the third gives federal recognition to the Little Shell Tribe of Chippewa Indians in Montana
- Trump finalized the creation of the Space Force as our 6th Military branch

- Trump signed a law to make cruelty to animals a federal felony so that animal abusers face tougher consequences
- Violent crime has fallen every year he's been in office after rising during the two years before he was elected
- Trump signed a bill making CBD and Hemp legal
- Trump's EPA gave $100 million to fix the water infrastructure problem in Flint, Michigan
- Under Trump's leadership, in 2018 the US surpassed Russia and Saudi Arabia to become the world's largest producer of crude oil
- Trump signed a law ending the gag orders on pharmacists that prevented them from sharing money-saving information
- Trump signed the "Allow States and Victims to Fight Online Sex Trafficking Act" (FOSTA), which includes the 'Stop Enabling Sex Traffickers Act' (SESTA) which both give law enforcement and victims new tools to fight sex trafficking
- Trump signed a bill to require airports to provide spaces for breastfeeding mothers
- The 25% lowest-paid Americans enjoyed a 4.5% income boost in November 2019, which outpaces a 2.9% gain in earnings for the country's highest-paid workers
- Low-wage workers are benefiting from higher minimum wages and from corporations that are increasing entry-level pay
- Trump signed the biggest wilderness protection and conservation bill in a decade and designated 375,000 acres as protected land
- Trump signed the Save our Seas Act which funds $10 million per year to clean plastic and garbage from the ocean
- He signed a bill this year allowing some drug imports from Canada so that prescription prices would go down
- Trump signed an executive order this year that forces all healthcare providers to disclose the cost of their services so that Americans can compare shops and know how much less providers charge insurance companies
- When signing that bill, he said no American should be blindsided by bills for medical services they never agreed to in advance

- Hospitals will now be required to post their standard charges for services, which include the discounted price a hospital is willing to accept
- In the eight years prior to President Trump's inauguration, prescription drug prices increased by an average of 3.6% per year Under Trump, drug prices have seen year-over-year de-clines in nine of the last ten months, with a 1.1% drop as of the most recent month
- He created a White House VA Hotline to help veterans and principally staffed it with veterans and direct family members of veterans
- VA employees are being held accountable for poor performance, with more than 4,000 VA employees removed, demoted, and suspended so far
- Issued an executive order requiring the Secretaries of Defence, Homeland Security, and Veterans Affairs to submit a joint plan to provide veterans access to access to mental health treatment as they transition to civilian life
- Because of a bill signed and championed by Trump, in 2020, most federal employees will see their pay increase by an average of 3.1% — the largest raise in more than ten years
- Trump signed into a law up to twelve weeks of paid parental leave for millions of federal workers
- The Trump administration will provide HIV prevention drugs for free to 200,000 uninsured patients per year for twelve years
- All-time record sales during the 2019 holidays
- Trump signed an order allowing small businesses to group together when buying insurance to get a better price
- President Trump signed the Preventing Maternal Deaths Act that provides funding for states to develop maternal mortality reviews to better understand maternal complications and identify solutions & largely focuses on reducing the higher mortality rates for Black Americans
- In 2018, President Trump signed the ground breaking First Step Act, a criminal justice bill which enacted reforms that make our justice system fairer and help former inmates successfully return to society
- The First Step Act's reforms addressed inequities in sentencing laws that disproportionately harmed Black Americans and reformed mandatory minimums that created unfair outcomes

- The First Step Act expanded judicial discretion in sentencing of non-violent crimes.
- Over 90% of those benefiting from the retroactive sentencing reductions in the First Step Act are Black Americans
- The First Step Act provides rehabilitative programs to inmates, helping them successfully rejoin society and not return to crime
- Trump increased funding for Historically Black Colleges and Universities (HBCUs) by more than 14%
- Trump signed legislation forgiving Hurricane Katrina debt that threatened HBCUs.
- New single-family home sales are up 31.6% in October 2019 compared to just one year ago
- Made HBCUs a priority by creating the position of executive director of the White House Initiative on HBCUs
- Trump received the Bipartisan Justice Award at a historically black college for his criminal justice reform accomplishments
- The poverty rate fell to a 17-year low of 11.8% under the Trump administration as a result of a jobs-rich environment
- Poverty rates for African-Americans and Hispanic-Americans have reached their lowest levels since the US began collecting such data
- President Trump signed a bill that creates five national monuments, expands several national parks, adds 1.3 million acres of wilderness, and permanently reauthorizes the Land and Water Conservation Fund
- Trump's USDA committed $124 Million to rebuild rural water infrastructure
- Consumer confidence & small business confidence is at an all-time high
- More than seven million jobs created since the election
- More Americans are now employed than ever recorded before in our history
- More than 400,000 manufacturing jobs have been created since his election
- Trump appointed five openly gay ambassadors
- Trump ordered Ric Grenell, his openly gay ambassador to Germany, to lead a global initiative to decriminalize homosexuality across the globe

- Through Trump's Anti-Trafficking Coordination Team (AC- Team) initiative, Federal law enforcement more than doubled convictions of human traffickers and increased the number of defendants charged by 75% in AC Team districts
- In 2018, the Department of Justice (DOJ) dismantled an organization that was the internet's leading source of prostitution-related advertisements resulting in sex trafficking
- Trump's OMB published new anti-trafficking guidance for government procurement officials to more effectively combat human trafficking
- Trump's Immigration and Customs Enforcement's Homeland Security Investigations arrested 1,588 criminals associated with human trafficking
- Trump's Department of Health and Human Services provided funding to support the National Human Trafficking Hotline to identify perpetrators and give victims the help they need
- The hotline identified 16,862 potential human trafficking cases
- Trump's DOJ provided grants to organizations that support human trafficking victims – serving nearly 9,000 cases from July 1, 2017, to June 30, 2018
- The Department of Homeland Security has hired more victim assistance specialists, helping victims get resources and support
- President Trump has called on Congress to pass school choice legislation so that no child is trapped in a failing school because of his or her zip code
- The president signed funding legislation in September 2018 that increased funding for school choice by $42 million
- The tax cuts signed into law by President Trump promote school choice by allowing families to use 529 college savings plans for elementary and secondary education
- Under his leadership ISIS has lost most of their territory and been largely dismantled
- ISIS leader Abu Bakr Al-Baghdadi was killed
- Signed the first Perkins CTE reauthorization since 2006, authorizing more than $1 billion for states each year to fund vocational and career education programs

- Executive order expanding apprenticeship opportunities for students and workers
- Trump issued an Executive Order prohibiting the US government from discriminating against Christians or punishing expressions of faith
- Signed an executive order that allows the government to withhold money from college campuses deemed to be anti-Semitic and who fail to combat anti-Semitism
- President Trump ordered a halt to US tax money going to international organizations that fund or perform abortions
- Trump imposed sanctions on the socialists in Venezuela who have killed their citizens
- Finalized new trade agreement with South Korea
- Made a deal with the European Union to increase US energy exports to Europe
- Withdrew the US from the job-killing TPP deal
- Secured $250 billion in new trade and investment deals in China and $12 billion in Vietnam
- Agreed up to $12 billion in aid for farmers affected by unfair trade retaliation
- Has had over a dozen US hostages freed, including those Obama could not get freed
- Trump signed the Music Modernization Act, the biggest change to copyright law in decades
- Trump secured billions that will fund the building of a wall at our southern border
- The Trump Administration is promoting second chance hiring to give former inmates the opportunity to live crime-free lives and find meaningful employment
- Trump's DOJ and the Board of Prisons launched a new 'Ready to Work Initiative' to help connect employers directly with former prisoners
- President Trump's historic tax cut legislation included new Opportunity Zone Incentives to promote investment in low-income communities across the country

- 8,764 communities across the country have been designated as Opportunity Zones
- Opportunity Zones are expected to spur $100 billion in long-term private capital investment in economically distressed communities across the country
- Trump directed the Education Secretary to end Common Core
- Trump signed the 9/11 Victims Compensation Fund into law
- Trump signed measure funding prevention programs for Veteran suicide
- Companies have brought back over a trillion dollars from overseas because of the TCJA bill that Trump signed
- Manufacturing jobs are growing at the fastest rate in more than thirty years
- Median household income has hit the highest level ever recorded
- African-American unemployment is at an all-time low
- Hispanic-American unemployment is at an all-time low
- Asian-American unemployment is at an all-time low
- Women's unemployment rate is at a 65-year low
- Youth unemployment is at a 50-year low
- We have the lowest unemployment rate ever recorded
- The pledge to America's workers has resulted in employers committing to train more than 4 million Americans
- 95% of US manufacturers are optimistic about the future—the highest ever
- As a result of the Republican tax bill, small businesses will have the lowest top marginal tax rate in more than 80 years
- Record number of regulations eliminated that hurt small businesses
- Signed welfare reform requiring able-bodied adults who don't have children to work or look for work if they're on welfare
- Under Trump, the FDA approved more affordable generic drugs than ever before in history
- Reformed Medicare program to stop hospitals from overcharging low-income seniors on their drugs—saving seniors hundreds of millions worth of dollars this year alone

- Signed Right-To-Try legislation allowing terminally ill patients to try experimental treatment that wasn't allowed before
- Secured $6 billion in new funding to fight the opioid epidemic
- Signed VA Choice Act and VA Accountability Act, expanded VA tele-health services, walk-in-clinics, and same-day urgent primary and mental health care
- US oil production recently reached all-time high so we are less dependent on oil from the Middle East
- The US is a net natural gas exporter for the first time since 1957
- NATO allies increased their defence spending because of his pressure campaign
- Withdrew the United States from the job-killing Paris Climate Accord in 2017 and that same year the US still led the world by having the largest reduction in Carbon emissions
- Has his circuit court judge nominees being confirmed faster than any other new administration
- The confirmation of both Supreme Court Justice's Neil Gorsuch and Brett Kavanaugh
- Moved US Embassy in Israel to Jerusalem
- Agreed to a new trade deal with Mexico & Canada that will increase jobs here and money coming in
- Reached a breakthrough agreement with the EU to increase US exports
- Imposed tariffs on China in response to China's forced technology transfer, intellectual property theft, and their chronically abusive trade practices, has agreed to a Part One trade deal with China
- Signed legislation to improve the National Suicide Hotline
- Signed the most comprehensive childhood cancer legislation ever into law, which will advance childhood cancer research and improve treatments
- The Tax Cuts and Jobs Act signed into law by Trump doubled the maximum amount of the child tax credit available to parents and lifted the income limits so more people could claim it
- It also created a new tax credit for other dependents
- In 2018, President Trump signed into law a $2.4 billion funding increase

for the Child Care and Development Fund, providing a total of $8.1 billion to States to fund child care for low-income families

- The Child and Dependent Care Tax Credit (CDCTC) signed into law by Trump provides a tax credit equal to 20-35% of child care expenses, $3,000 per child & $6,000 per family plus Flexible Spending Accounts (FSAs) allow you to set aside up to $5,000 in pre-tax dollars to use for child care

- In 2019 President Donald Trump signed the Autism Collaboration, Accountability, Research, Education and Support Act (CARES) into law which allocates $1.8 billion in funding over the next five years to help people with autism spectrum disorder and to help their families

- In 2019 President Trump signed into law two funding packages providing nearly $19 million in new funding for Lupus specific research and education programs, as well an additional $41.7 billion in funding for the National Institutes of Health (NIH), the most Lupus funding ever

- The US stock market continually hits all-time record highs Trump did all of this while fighting flagrant abuse and impeachment charges. As November 2020 approaches, although hardly any of his executive orders and accomplishments would make it to mainstream media, Trump's achievements are a reminder that Trump and his team are doing real things that have real impact on real lives. The president's achievements explain why the policies are gaining him an army of new recruits of supporters, who are all solidly behind him

5

MAINSTREAM MEDIA THE ENEMY OF THE PEOPLE

The media bias and double standards were obvious to all by the end of 2018 and the Democrats and their supporters have taken full advantage of it, as they have continued in their relentless attacks.

All through the novel pandemic, even the experts were making and continuing giving varied changing advice – not their fault because even the world knew that it was a new type of virus, but the left-leaning mainstream media were simply hostile and belligerent whenever the president relied on their expert advice. In the UK, Piers Morgan led the attacks and many other journalists followed, as they baited the people to demand to sack various ministers and secretaries in Mr Johnson's cabinet.

On October 29th, 2013 Hilary Clinton said, "I don't know what it is exactly about him, I can't quite put my finger on it, but my instinct is almost never wrong. And it's telling me that Donald Trump would be very successful if he were to venture into politics in the future."

Two-thirds of voters now believe major news organizations have political agenda and many believe that most reporters are trying to block President Trump's agenda and that the mainstream media have lost their standards.

MEDIA ENGAGEMENT BAITING

Quite simply, the mainstream media, including most chat groups in particular Facebook and Twitter, put out information based at least in part on actual information embedded with fake news edits in order to trap and engage the audience for a response. The journalists simply think that many people are nonetheless inclined to believe them and as such, the president has called them the 'enemies of the people', mainly because not only is propaganda objectionable, but this propaganda is objectionable, because it is anti-democratic propaganda.

My suspicions and concerns about the mainstream media and their relationship with the president started quite soon after the inauguration, when the media frenzy was that the First Lady (FLOTUS) had stolen Jackie Kennedy's look in that stunning blue outfit from decades ago – that got my attention – a simple research showed that the only likeness was the corn flour blue colour. The style of the outfit was totally dissimilar – I felt that I had probably not understood the media report – and let that one go.

It was when 12-year old Baron was pictured asleep with the salacious comments about being 'bored and ill-mannered to sleep through the very hectic day' that I just concluded that there were some dark forces at work.

Then the memes arrived showing that FLOTUS Melania had plagiarised a speech that former FLOTUS Michelle delivered back in 2008. I was excited at that piece of news, shared it and reposted it. When that news persisted, I then decided to research on both speeches in order to have a better belly laugh – that soon turned to misgiving and mistrust for the press and shame for joining in the mob hate after I eventually found the matching phrases from the two speeches and found only three word –integrity, compassion and intelligence – the reasons for the overblown media reactions?

CORPORATE AGENDA

Over two thirds of voters now believe that the mainstream media have their own political agenda – and that is to block President Trump's policies and to deceive the American people. As far back in 2016, Donald J Trump was not popular with America's mainstream media and of the 100 top circulation print newspapers only two had endorsed him.

I was shocked to hear about and see the Antifa and Black Lives Matter rioting in the various Democrat run communities on social media. Everyone could see the violence, groups of agitators in their black outfits, helmets and their shields attacking the police, causing violence, throwing rocks but none of it is shown on mainstream media or the national news. Many people cannot see it, they do not know it, and most people do not even listen to the news but rely on verbal narratives. The corporate media owners know this and that is part of their corporate agenda; the people must be left in darkness and all they need to know about politics is that Trump is racist as embarrassingly touched on by even most of my reasonably educated friends and family.

Right from the 2016 campaigns days few people realised that the mainstream media would not cover his speeches or policies apart from the transmissions from the leftist media. Trump countered this unfair treatment by resorting to social media – following his posts and those of the White House means you get the information directly from the sources.

'Fake news' and deliberate disinformation continued to spread via traditional news media and the various online social media.

The mainstream media feed on stoking fear and race hate and have become a sad example of poor journalism.

Since Trump declared to run for office, they have been relentless in pushing false doomsday scenarios to attack the president.

Most of the presidents' valuable time has been spent disproving and invalidating the fake news; it rarely gets retracted and even when they do, the people have few or no chances of seeing it refuted. With very few apologies many are left with the memory and belief of the biased news.

The curious thing is that when the president exposes the hoax via his tweets or through other news feeds or blogs, the previously hourly looped news abruptly stops being reported, without any corrections and never an apology – well, my research found none, all of which made me understand why the president called the media the "enemy of the people" in 2017. This had elicited outrage. Arizona Republican Senator Jeff Flake said it was an example of an 'unprecedented' and 'unwarranted' White House assault on the free press. He calls them 'lame stream' media – a pun on the word 'mainstream' media, which reminds people to fact check and not to trust the media.

The media played a direct role in Donald Trump's 2016 election success and they will be doing it again in November 2020 because many undecided voters are finding the many fabrications and insults hurled at the president and his family inappropriate and uncalled for. The worm is now turning – the fact of the matter is that the president depends on chaos, insults and fake news to increase his support base – because it makes them investigate or research more from being inquisitive in order to discover the truth.

The point here is that the media has relied on the president's unique correct type of enemies that necessitates a one-party media: the pundits, the 'social scientists' and the righteous fear mongers, all of which are easy pickings and great for their ratings.

Trump's victory, then, was a brutal kick and a humiliating blow for the thousands of journalists who had spent months trying to warn the public that a vote for Donald J Trump would be a waste of time.

The president still needs to relay his message and policies whenever the opportunity presents itself in speeches, at events or visits which has not stopped the media from editing his messages by splicing words and even full sentences out with such negative vengeful force.

What is left is an 'angry' hostile media scavenging in wait each day for Trump's tweets in which to dissect and publish. Trump means ratings and the unpredictable and ever telegenic president, will have the cameras and ratings continually following wherever he goes.

The haters end up making him a winner when they share and spread the post around like a virus and even get converted to his policies whenever they bother to seek the original source. The Trump base has grown mostly because Trump although distracted and time consuming, the president has continued to correct most of the negative, incessant and breathless attacks on everything he does.

There are many instances of deliberate false statements, and as recent as April 2020, anti-Trump HBO host Bill Maher warned the establishment media that their dishonest and sensational reporting during the coronavirus pandemic might help President Donald Trump get reelected.

Another prominent producer, MSNBC producer quit on July 24 2020 and published a resignation letter criticizing the network and the journalism industry as a whole. Ariana Pekary had been a producer at MSNBC since 2013 and wrote that,

"The problem is the job itself. It forces skilled journalists to make bad decisions on a daily basis…all the commercial networks function the same."

Pekary said that during her time at the network, she saw decisions on news content were based on how a topic or guest would 'rate'.

BIAS AND ENTRAPMENT

It has been known that whenever a presidential election looms, the media tends to have serious sexual accusations to add to the melee most of which are revealed as made up but rarely retracted.

In late April 2020, many on Twitter rebuked Hilary Clinton and the 'Me Too Movement' over Tara Reade, a former Senate staffer for enabling sexual predators.

Reade had claimed that her former boss, Joe Biden had touched and raped her.

"I voted for Hillary Clinton in 2016. I voted for her in the primary

Reade had commented. "Hillary Clinton has a history of enabling powerful men to cover up their sexual predatory behaviours and their inappropriate sexual misconduct… I will not be smeared, dismissed or ignored. I stand in truth and I will keep speaking out" she said.

Another instance of how the mainstream media go after the Republicans in fact, indirectly at the president, is again demonstrated in the Democrats' failed attempt to get Brett Michael Kavanaugh, an American lawyer and Associate Justice of the Supreme Court of the United States.

Before Judge Kavanaugh could take up the vacant seat, he had to be approved by the 21-strong Senate Judiciary Committee and then the whole Senate.

Then out of the blues, came accusations of sexual attacks some thirty years back, in a teenagers' drunken party that none of them remembered enough details of who, what and when it all happened. The judge has denied both allegations, labelling the latest "a smear", but this did not stop the 'Me Too' crowd out in full weeks of media barrage and street protests.

Contrast this to Joe Biden who still faces serious sexual assault charges against a lady Tara Reade– but the mainstream media are not covering the news. There was even more proof of this, a video was found where a story was published about the Biden sexual as-sault that happened some thirty years ago when Tara Reade worked for Joe Biden for eight months and was persistently touched and grabbed. She was actually attacked and assaulted in a corridor.

Biden is backed by the mainstream media, Hollywood and Soros, so, not a single comment from either the movement or from the mainstream media has been made on behalf of Tara Reade.

The Hollywood and Soros sponsored 'Me Too movement' protesters did not make a single comment, no rude protesters in Trafalgar square, no Media frenzy – just media blank out on the story. The Me Too (or #MeToo) movement, is a movement set up to support women that have claimed sexual harassment and sexual assault especially in the workplace. Following the exposure of the widespread sexual-abuse allegations against Harvey Weinstein in early October 2018, the movement began to spread virally as a hashtag on social media. American actress Alyssa Milano posted on Twitter, "If all the women who have been sexually harassed or assaulted wrote 'Me Too' as a status, we might give people a sense of the magnitude of the problem.

George Soros, the Hungarian-American billionaire investor is reported to have bankrolled the 'MeToo' movement – set up to attack right-wing people.

MEDIA FRENZY TACTICS

Typically, the press had several attack plans.

It almost always starts off with the Democrat politicians giving snippets of hate to the press. They are then paid by their sponsors and donors to use whatever tactics at their disposal to hound Trump and this has left a dreadful stain on journalism.

Trump has been the target of a vicious and orchestrated campaign of hate from the day of his inauguration. Their usual strategy is to play out and roll over every word or sentence uttered from the president for as long as another spin can be used.

The most common plan is used by reporters. The reporters may highlight a sentence and ignore the next sentence, ignore the mid-sentence and possibly ignore the first word, or even ignore the last words or even both, hence taking an important comment out of context.

It is usually the more discerning viewers that bother to find the original statement in order to make their own informed judgment.

The mainstream media write whatever they want, seldom have sources (even though they say they do), never do "fact checking" anymore, and are only looking for the "kill" – here I mean take good news and make it bad, making them beyond fake, but corrupt.

The Democrats and mainstream media pin their hopes on the fact that the people would forget, so, as soon as they get caught out, they abruptly end that line of attack, with no apologies and move to a new scheme and of course.

The past four years have seen mainstream presenters completely obsessing with opposing anything Trump says or does in order to delay him from exposing the Democrats most of whom have invested in companies and are on the board of companies within Trump's radar for corruption and even strategies that put the America peoples' lives in danger.

During briefings the reporters always come armed with their scheming lists of 'gotcha' questions in hopes of improving their personal popularity for social media. This always backfires because

Trump loves to talk, a very great leadership asset. He knows his stuff so well that the briefings put him in his element where he responds astutely to every question and more.

Soon after the pandemic lockdown, the president's support base were no longer taking the media reports seriously – the focus was on how the policies were going to save lives and make things better; and the ratings of CNN, nicknamed Clinton News Network, or the Chinese News Network had continued to plummet, so were our ITV, LBC and BBC as both Trump haters and supports were advising and comforting all to stop listening to the mainstream media, which much of this ratings dive more from the Democrat's supporters.

In today's age of social media and ever-expanding knowledge, people need to be well informed on the happenings in the world around them so as not to be totally ignorant to the events outside of themselves and their space in life. This is, however, difficult to do with snippets of news continually leaked to the mainstream media for broadcast or as we have all seen, to be used for 'got cha' questioning moments. I kept pondering on how it could happen until I discovered that several politicians are in fact physically and literally married to media personnel. For instance;

- Susan Rice and Ian Cameron are married, but Cameron left ABC News at the end of 2010 after spending thirteen years with the organization. Cameron said he wanted a job that al-lowed him to spend more time with his family.
- CBS President David Rhodes and Ben Rhodes, a deputy national security advisor to President Obama, are brothers. The connection between the brothers drew criticism after CBS

Evening News opted not to report on an email written by Ben Rhodes that reportedly demonstrated how the Obama administration had shaped talking points surrounding the deadly attacks in Benghazi in 2012.

- Reporter Matthew Jaffe, a reporter for ABC News and Univision, and Katie Hogan were married in 2012.
- ABC President Ben Sherwood and Elizabeth Sherwood, special advisor to President Obama, are siblings. Elizabeth Sherwood was named as the White House coordinator for defence policy, weapons of mass destruction and arms control in March of 2013.
- CNN's Virginia Moseley is married to former Deputy Secretary Tom Nides.

The list goes on, but it helps one to put things into perspective. In effect, the politicians could easily leak snippets to the media, who are meant to spin it all out for broadcasting.

As I researched further, I began to see another pattern of how comments disguised as leaks were fed to the media which also made me realise that the Democrats were becoming desperate. They tended to use anti-Trump twitter or face book posts to set up the attack, feed it to the media who then spring it on President Trump in interviews. For instance, on the May 9th 2020, Obama was reported to have described President Trump's exemplary and tireless effort on the corona pandemic as 'an absolute chaotic disaster'. My theory was right; the comments were made while privately talking to ex-members of his administration, which was leaked to Yahoo News.

With mostly only bias and even hate most of the time, like millions of others, I simply listen to the news headlines for the topics to possibly research on and when the likes of BBC Naga Munchetty or Louise Minchin come on air – I switch off, as many other viewers have commented and eventually ended up with Bill Turnbull on Classic FM.

FAKE NEWS AND DISINFORMATION

Whenever I asked around to know why there was such an inordinate amount of hate, the response was almost always – 'don't you listen to the news?' I have always been a BBC ITV person, but soon found CNN on Sky 505. I could not quite make out the reporters without subtitles, and resorted to rewinding several times in order to read and make sense of the very short sentences.

Purely by chance, I found someone had posted something about 'Trump's amazing rally' in a Facebook post and my search came up with Right Side Broadcasting Network (RSBN) that covered the rallies in detail, and of lately One America News Network (OANN) recommended by the president.

My own personal experience with the fake news media was when president trump visited the UK and the media claimed that there were a handful of Trump supporters. That was totally false. I was there – I had taken photographs that proved otherwise. We were not as the organised protesters who were allowed to gather to form a crowd and trudge down Whitehall from Trafalgar Square. There were pockets of Trump supporters penned up at various locations not to mention those that stood around disguised as mere spectators that could have easily topped 10,000.

The CNN news was a complete no! no! After the pain of trying to watch for several weeks, I could never get used to their broadcast intonation. As if that was not enough, in desperation I decided to try one of their audience news shows and came across one hosted by Seth Myers. I did try, honestly, I did try to watch that most odious man which I found so painful and irritating but after watching six consecutive recorded shows I simply had it removed that most insufferable show from my series-link recordings.

NOTHING TO SPIN? – MAKE IT UP

Various political critics, journalists, and in particular failing celebrities have continued to use Trump to be relevant. They have also continued goading – and we all know how it ends – it all backfires with the proverbial 'hands of God' and with no involvement from the president.

When the media run low on scraps of news, they simply make it up. In late April 2020 CNN host Don Lemon quipped on air

What is it about President Obama that really gets under your skin?

Is it because he's smarter than you?

Better educated? Made it on his own? Didn't need Daddy's help?

Wife is more accomplished? Better looking?

I don't know, what is it? What is it about him?

That he's a black man that's accomplished being president?

That he punked you on the whole birth certificate thing?

What is it about him? Just wondering.

With the above, the president did not respond. Any form of attack on FLOTUS really does rile up the Trump supporters.

What happened next was a barrage of social media artillery launched in response – this was really wicked, a meme of a very 'butch' looking Michelle Obama went viral – the haters immediately stopped responding.

One Rick Wilson, a former GOP Political strategist and well known for his anti-Trump rhetoric wished coronavirus infection on FLOTUS Melania, just like that, all because the first lady had an anti-bullying campaign. CNN had aired his hate comment and felt that it was quite alright rather than sickening to apparently decide during a pandemic that it was all right to joke that FLOTUS should be a victim of the coronavirus because of her 'Be Best campaign'.

Rick Wilson, I discovered, is a very famous Anti-Trump CNN Pundit and had spent the past four years attacking President Trump and his supporters. He was famously seen on set with CNN's Don Lemon, where they both played out an exaggerated belly-laugh insult on the president, there was no insult to make up that day. The attacks and laughing went on for some five minutes and a few days later, the hands of God struck.

The revenge came when it was revealed that not only did Rick Wilson's wife post photos of her 'confederate beach cooler' with the words, '...the South Will Rise Again', on her Instagram account several years ago – not only that, back in 2011, Molly had tweeted that, "...this is going to sound bad...But I need some Mexicans for about three days to work in my garden. #overgrown."

Confirming that for her, Mexicans are 'helps', and merely servants. The people did not forget and Trump's fans shredded and roasted Rick Wilson and his wife's on social media with reprisals that made his wife Molly 'lockdown' her Twitter account.

Rick Wilson used to be a Republicans with a new book in production. It will be interesting to see whether Rick Wilson will remain at CNN – he has been quite absent for several months now, I hear.

George Soros is not the only one to sponsor attacks on the president. Several people had paid and are still funding groups to attack the president. As far back as December 31st, 2017 it was reported that a Hillary Clinton 'backer' had paid $500,000 to fund women accusing Trump of sexual misconduct before the 2016 Elections.

Susie Tompkins Buell, the founder of Esprit Clothing and a major Clinton campaign donor for many years is one of these backers. She gave the money to celebrity lawyer Lisa Bloom who was working with a number of Trump accusers at the time, Bloom worked for four women who were considering accusing Trump, in the end, two went public, and two declined.

Bloom had solicited donors by saying she was working with women who might 'find the courage to speak out' against Trump if the donors would provide funds for security, relocation and possibly a 'safe house,' the paper reported.

David Brock, a political consultant and author also donated. He fell for the scam and paid $200,000.

One of the women demanded $2 million for the scam and then decided not to come forward. Nor did any other women.

Bloom said she refunded most of the cash, keeping only some funds for out-of-pocket expenses accrued while working to coach the plant accusers and prepare the cases but never offered money to coax or coach the women.

Bloom had even arranged for a donor to pay off the mortgage of one of Trump's accusers in her desperate bid to entrap the president. The woman with the mortgage ultimately declined to come forward after being offered $750,000.

From my analysis above, the Democrats need the minority Americans to remain in a permanent ignorant oppressed state to benefit from their votes. What you have, through no fault of theirs, is a voter base so ill-informed that even when their candidates promise to raise their taxes, and leave their borders unprotected, they will still vote for them because they have been conditioned to do so by the media.

When I requested to know why the media was so hateful, I was almost always referred to an Obama birth certificate issue – for asking Obama to produce his birth certificate. The mainstream media had looped the furore for months.

As it is, only US-born people can be president of the United States, and Obama had taken an inordinate length of time to produce the document when the inquiry commenced. So, in April 2011, President Barack Obama sought to put an end to rumours claiming that he was a natural-born citizen of the United States by obtaining and releasing a copy of his long form birth certificate issued by the state of Hawaii, after years of calling the request 'silly'.

If the truth be told, even British birth certificates can be and has been known to be forged and bought. Obama should have been made to produce backup documentation such as a baptism certificate or medical card usually issued within days of birth – research cannot confirm whether Obama managed to produce any accompanying documents.

In effect, the mainstream media succeeded in creating a voter base that is so bitter with hate for a president that even when a candidate promises to raise their taxes, disarm them, leave their borders open and unprotected they still vote for the candidate.

6

KU KLUX KLAN (KKK) AGENDA

I was shocked to discover that the Democrat 'icon' Robert Byrd, who died nine years ago, was a Grand Wizard of the Ku Klux Klan (the KKK). Founded in 1865, the Ku Klux Klan (KKK) became the Democrat's vehicle to attack the Republicans policies aimed at establishing political and economic equality for Black Americans.

Who would have guessed that speaker Nancy Pelosi had attended her good friend and Robert Byrd's funeral nine years ago which she revealed in her opening speech,

"I bring, as Speaker of the House, I sadly have the privilege of bringing the condolences of the House of Representatives to Marjorie and to Mona and the entire Byrd family. As a friend of Senator Byrd, I do so with great sadness. But happily, thanks to the Byrd family, some of us had the opportunity to sing Senator Byrd's praises in his presence in December, when he became the longest-serving Member of Congress in American history."

Joe Biden was at the funeral as well as Obama and Clinton. Understandably, historically, the Democrats were the slave owning masters and the Republicans were the ones that sought to abolish slavery with the help of my ancestors at Onitsha in Nigeria.

The present-day Democrats now accuse President Trump of being a 'racist' and his supporters as 'Nazis.' As they try to drown their own racist identity with the mainstream media:

- 18th century slaves were prevented from thinking for themselves
- 22nd century black American prevented themselves from thinking for themselves using the mainstream media (CNN and MSNBC in particular) to feed us their editorialised re-ports and Fake News
- 18th century slaves were dependent on slave owners for food and housing
- 22nd Century Black American dependent on welfare for food and housing
- 18th century slaves needed by the Democrats to increase their wealth
- 22nd century black American votes needed by the Democrats to increase their wealth

They do not stop there, they use the media to encourage division, rioting and violent mobs to tear down Confederate statues – which ironically, are all part of the Democrat Party history. Meanwhile they are praying that as many of the mob are as ignorant to know that the person funding all these extreme left socialist attacks is Soros. He continues to bribe the mainstream media to distract the people with continuous media coverage of one episode after the other to subdue the black American, convincing them that they are an oppressed race.

There have been several blasts played out on mainstream media between the president and several black celebrities. Many people do not realise or may have forgotten that the president was brought up in Queens, New York and as a child, his parents packed him off to military school – where he met with a lot of other 'toughies' – and he took up wrestling and was highly respected to be made team leader.

With that in mind, anyone can understand how he keeps going on and can take on any politician, including several snivelling 'celebrities' and news reporters sponsored by Soros to be Trump haters.

The president as we have seen has always managed to get even one way or the other with his political adversaries and the media, most of the time by the proverbial hand of God and rarely directly, as I found in the façade that involved the media and various personalities.

This is demonstrated in several very high-profile events such as the Jussie Smollett alleged assault, the Lebron James foul-up, Colin Rand Kaepernick, Bubba Wallace and lately, Black Lives Matters.

When Lebron, a black National Basketball Association (NBA) football player opened a school for underprivileged children in his hometown Akron, Ohio, all saw on August 4th, 2018, when the president tweeted, "I preferred to applaud Michael Jordan."

The mainstream media, Democrats and their supporters concluded that he was racist because he preferred Michael Jordan – who I also researched and noted that he too was a black American (netball) footballer.

My research found the source of the argument started as far back as September 2017, when Lebron James joined the stream of Trump celebrity haters and had disrespectfully called the President of his county a 'bum' and continued in a rancorous statement that,

---

"...going to the White House was a great honour until you showed up."

This led to a response from the former National Football League (NFL) super star – Herschel Walker,

He continued that he was in no way condoning the issue of racism in America, or police brutality. Like many people, he also would gladly protest. but will never ever disrespect the flag.

"President Trump is right when it comes to national anthem protests, the NFL needs to impose rules banning players from kneeling during the games."

As for being racist, Trump has continued to connect with the black community from day one, and did not wait for the crucial month leading to the elections as other politicians usually do.

Most of his economic policies never get aired on mainstream media, but they are there and they are experiencing the benefits and are talking about it and are defending him loud enough on social media.

I came across Byron Donalds, a Florida state representative and 19th congressional district Republican Conservative candidate for Congress. He stated that,

"...Trump Will 'Reap the Benefits' of Black Voter Outreach...the president has done a tremendous job. Probably the first president in my time that's actively tried to court and actually speak to minority voters, and black voters in particular."

From January 2020, one cannot read anything on social media without seeing liberal mainstream media minions regurgitating disinformation or just by default trashing anything the administration does especially when the President had shown exceptional leadership in unifying the nation especially in trying to support, embrace as many back people as he can and break the black peoples conditioned response to hate everything with a conservative ideology.

WHY THEY HATE TRUMP

President Trump has seen an inordinate increase in his support base, and many on group chats have acclaimed that although they did not vote for him in 2016, they love him and will vote for him in November 2020 simply because they say that he is a fighter, and that's exactly what America needs.

The president never minces his words, he talks straight, gets to the point and tells it like it is. Rancid as they are or not, Trump's politics don't seem to be the main reason he riles up so many liberals. I managed to purloin several statements from liberal chat group during my research on why many on the other hand do not like him,

"My wife likes his smile."

"He wears a wig."

"He lies constantly."

"He is a billionaire."

"He never pays taxes."

"We do not like his wife – she is pretty."

"I did not like the show."

"He cannot sing."

Women think he looks attractive."

"He makes the news."

"He eats burgers."

"He is not a conventional politician." "The president is not diplomatic when hespeaks."

"Trump dates and marries trophyladies." "His cabinet picks, know significantly less about the world than Obama's did or Hillary's wouldhave."

"My wife thinks he looks attractive with the COVID mask on!"

"We want free health for all illegal immigrants"

"We want free college for all illegal immigrants"

"Trump keeps provoking war indirectly because some countries do not like his personality', (despite even Iran backed down and is playing ball with UN and US – this was from a Mark Kaye online Show phone in)

"He got married twice"

"It doesn't matter unemployment down"

"It doesn't matter that he has faced up to China"

"It doesn't matter that he prompted peace withKorea"

"He did not pay his taxes in 2016 and 2017" – at this I reposted on social media that he may have even claimed rebates from the taxman. Here in the UK, it is a common basic accounting task to ensure that business owners offset income in one asset with expenses in another – every day accounting work! My field in finance.

These responses are endemic among Democrat supporters and the only cure after months of intense hate is to try to save face after all those months of retching out deranged hate as directed by the mainstream media. As such, many are jumping ship in support of the president, while others – with Masters degrees etc, simply re-affirm without thinking or researching 'we just want him out' – based on news reports.

DEMOCRAT AGENDA WITH CELEBRITIES

Currently loved and loathed in equal measure, before he became president, most of them were his friends, and the sudden switch to hate can only be jealousy. With the knowledge that he has far outclassed their celebrity status to becoming a world-class personality and the most powerful person on Earth.

President Trump still has his celebrity friends who have not only stood by him but have been vocal in their support – such as Jon Voight, Kelsey Grammer, Kid Rock, Stacey Dash, Clint Eastwood and many more.

However, there are the many fading celebrities set about being vocal against the president, although most, if not all of the key players had at one time or the other sought favours from him before he became president. In their attempts to get back in the spotlight or to get some publicity, they have not held back in lashing out at the president.

Trump knows where they are all coming from, and knows where all the bodies are buried. Most of the time, he ignores them and then sits back for their comeuppance through that proverbial hand of God.

Three notable organisations; '#UnitedAgainstHate', 'MoveOn. Org' and of lately 'MeToo' have since declined in popularity and interest especially after Soros plugged off his sponsorship funds. They community platforms set up to start petitions, organized supporters, engaged decision-makers, and won their own grassroots campaigns particularly directed against Trump and all his supporters.

The signatories shamelessly include high profile actors, producers, directors, comedians, screenwriters, musicians and fashion designers across the country.

We all know how silent and invisible the 'Me Too' movement has been on behalf of Tara Reade, because Biden is a democrat, backed and protected by the mainstream media, Hollywood and Soros.

After Trump won in 2016, and proved them all wrong for wasting their time and money, their embarrassment turned to relentless bile. Several have realised that they were taken in and have kept a dignified silence, but quite a few others have remained relentlessly bitter and twisted using Climate change and emissions of carbon dioxide as the basis for their hate. These celebrities with their hypocrisies include, Whoopi Goldberg, Oprah Winfrey not to mention the former duchess of Sussex Meghan Markle whose groundless hate against the president caused social media backlash here in the UK. Like most of the personalities, she too is still receiving her just deserts without the president lifting a finger.

Many other self-made celebrities have come up in support of the president. Celebrities such as Shaquille O'Neal, Floyd Mayweather, Herschel Walker, Jeannie Pierro, boxing legend Mike Tyson, Stacey Dash, Kanye West have stated that quite simply, celebrities should not coerce or tell people who to vote for. Candace Amber Owens-Farmer the black American conservative political activist was to comment,

"For the people who fly private but lecture us about the environment, for the people who live in gated communities but lecture us about building walls, to the people who travel with armed guards and lecture us about guns, your bottomless hypocrisy is why America choses Trump."

What we are now seeing is that the president rarely needs to unleash his fire storm these days on the haters. Apart from his army base of supporters who do the fighting on his behalf, there is a limit to what they can do to create such an impact hit, which is why I feel it's a sort of divine intervention to help the president.

Ricky Gervais the British Comedian was to rip the Hollywood elites in January 2020 that 'people are tired of being lectured to during quarantine'.

Here he was attacking celebrities that were posting photographs of themselves in lockdown,

"I've got nothing against anyone being a celebrity or being famous. I think that people are just a bit tired of being lectured to" Gervais had said.

Although the president has not retaliated, many hating high profile celebrities have fallen foul of the hand of God in defence of the president, and here are a few of them.

ELLEN DEGENERES

Ellen DeGeneres, who publicly flaunted her hate by stating continuously that she would never give President Trump an interview, has also received her own comeuppance.

In 2018, DeGeneres and Democrat Kamala Harris were on set having a good, hearty laugh about potentially doing away with Donald Trump — or Mike Pence, or Jeff Sessions.

The Ellen DeGeneres Show is reportedly under an internal investigation by Warner Media, the parent company to the show, as a result of multiple "toxic work environments" being brought to the public eye.

It has been reported that one current and ten former staff members have claimed to be victims of bullying and racism and the show is being axed.

COLIN RAND KAEPERNICK

The people who disrespect our flag foul up and the American football players' protests started in early 2016 when Colin Rand Kaepernick an American football player was sulking when he was sent off a game and in that ratty mood, decided to remain seated during the National Anthem.

Sitting down during the national anthem, was noticed by chance and this drew a lot of backlash on social media and as a damage limitation tactics, in August 2016, decided to kneel instead of stand during the national anthem, claiming that he was protesting against racism in America and police brutality against black people. The kneeling protest excuse was a good spin by his PR agents because it was clearly for a just cause, and by the end of September 2016, the kneeling fever gripped most if not all the American football players of America.

Many saw through the scam, but could not say much because the spin had 'racist' implications.

Everyone knows the love and protective nature that Trump has for disrespecting the flag or one of the armed forces and tweeted,

"NFL owners should fire the SOBS who disrespect our flag."

Nowhere in that tweet did Trump mention any particular race of SOB? His comment was not about race, it was about honouring the American flag, and in his opinion, anyone, any colour, any gender who disrespects the flag is a SOB.

The history about disrespecting the flag used to be peculiar in only developing countries where foreign yobs burn the flag; however, when 'American citizens' disrespect the American flag, the experience literally brings them down to the level of those yobbos.

LEBRON JAMES

In the orchestrated scheme by footballer Lebron James to publicise his educational complex for at-risk youth in Akron, Ohio, his PR consultants had suggested an interview with CNN during in order for the anchor to plug in a criticism of the president 'trying to divide the nation' and hopefully, any reaction from the president would be exaggerated to create news, in effect, the intended publicity.

The president had ignored them, however, they went further to call him a racist, because the tweet that he posted, following the disrespect to the US flag,

"NFL owners should fire the sobs who disrespect our flag."

Lebron James brought on the unprovoked attack when he went on to comment that 'the number one job in America ... is someone who doesn't understand the people, and really don't give a fuck about the people,' and that he was 'happy to use his fame to call out the president'.

Trump had kept a dignified silence, however, when from nowhere Don Lemon, the CNN anchor decided to complete the PR stunt, by stating that Trump was racist for caging children while Lebron was putting children in schools instead – that was not a personal attack but a blatant lie against Trump's policy and fuelling the race card, bound to create media hysteria and guaranteed to gain an onslaught from the president.

It is a known fact that many viewers do not research enough or at all on news broadcasts and the subsequent editorials.

All the viewers saw at the day was that Trump had singled out two adult black people and called them dumb when he responded and tweeted that,

"Lebron was just interviewed by the dumbest man on television, Don Lemon. He made Lebron look smart, which isn't easy to do. I like Mike!"

Don Lemon was to respond by stating that "the President traffics in racism and is fuelled by bullying." Don Lemon continued, "...the president's bullying is apparent from keeping children at the border in cages to bullying journalists at every one of his rallies and every chance he gets."

The cage incidents have been covered already but as a reminder the practice of separating and putting children in lock up centres, called cages, was set up by Obama in the previous administration as far back as 2013, years before Trump declared for office.

A few months later, Lebron would dishonourably disgrace himself – his hypocrisy would be exposed when it was revealed that here he was preaching about the importance of treating people fairly, and supporting riots of people rising up against "injustice," and they cheering on the removal of (Democrat) salve owner statues, all while wearing shoes and uniforms that are made in China by forced slave labour that is a perfect one to be remembered with in the history books(!)

This method of promoting either business, or temporarily increasing viewer ratings has continued, however, it is all leaning towards the president's re-election advantage as the truth gets revealed.

JUSSIE SMOLLETT

On January 29th, 2019, the black American actor Jussie Smollett went to the Chicago police to report that he was assaulted quite early in the morning by two people he described as white men, including MAGA references, thus directly attacking the president that was really immoral.

They had physically attacked him and had shouted racial and homophobic slurs at him, after having poured an unknown chemical substance on him and tied a noose around his neck.

There was such an attack by the media and Democrats all because the attackers were alleged to have worn Trump supporters' caps on. Race baiting has a very serious effect, even Smollett's cohost Grace Byers was to say,

"This despicable act only shamefully reveals how deeply the diseases of hatred, inequality, racism and discrimination continue to course through our country's veins."

On February 13th, 2019, Chicago police raided the home of two Nigerian-American brothers who had worked with Smollett as extras on the set of his television show. The brothers had been paid $3,500 by Smollett and had purchased the rope found around Smollett's neck. Smollett was indicted for disorderly conduct for allegedly paying the brothers to stage a fake hate crime assault on him and filing a false police report.

Apparently, Jussie Smollett had staged the hate crime because he had been written off the last season of the show 'Empire' – and he needed to improve his sunken image, by playing the race card with unfair references to the President for maximum impact. After the farce, he got away lightly, the charges were dropped because Jussie forfeited a $10,000 (£7,600) bail and carried out community service.

FREDO AFFAIR

And then, there was CNN's journalist Chris Cuomo notoriously ill-famed for his rabid attacks on the president caught on a viral video threatening to beat up a man who called him 'Fredo'.

It all happened when a fellow passenger believed his name to be Fredo. Cuomo related the name to Fredo Corleone, the dim-witted and disloyal older brother of Michael, the central character in the movie The Godfather.

In line with his CNN ego, Cuomo had taken it as an anti-Italian insult and threatened to throw the man down a flight of stairs, in the most vicious vulgar language while a cell phone camera captured the scene. In a futile damage limitation attempt, he claimed that the name 'Fredo' was 'the N-word for Italians'.

CNN and the Democrat supporters were left awfully 'embarrassed' by the viral Chris Cuomo video scandal. They reportedly tweeted that the incident gave ammunition to President Trump and as usual hoped for the week to go past so the people would forget.

In a later incident, the president hater had claimed to be under quarantine and had not seen his family in over two weeks, however, during that period, a cyclist revealed that he had seen Cuomo in public on Easter Sunday 2020 and questioned why he wasn't in quarantine since he had tested positive for the coronavirus instead of joy-riding about on his bicycle,

"You're breaking your brother's quarantine rules."

Cuomo was then said to say to him,

"Who the hell are you? I can do what I want!"

The 'bully' CNN anchor further launched a 'verbal attack' on him, and he reported him to police. He went on to say that Cuomo, who had tested positive for coronavirus, had ranted about his top post on telly at CNN.

Cuomo, a younger brother to the governor of New York was chastised by White House press secretary Kayleigh McEnany for taking President Trump's Hydroxychloroquine to handle his coronavirus infection after having condemned it on air as 'a beautiful distraction'.

ROSIE O'DONNELL

In 2016, Fox News host Megyn Kelly attacked Donald Trump during the first official presidential debate for 'demeaning comments he's made over the years about women', pointing out that he had in the past called women 'fat pigs' and 'slobs.'

Few of us knew the history behind the verbal lashings. The president had called out only one woman in particular, a top celebrity at the time, Rosie O'Donnell whom he had also called a 'real loser' and a 'woman out of control' after the comedienne mentioned "Trump and his daughter's weird relationship as bordering on the incestuous."

Many felt that Trump was rather lenient on her, however, the hand of God struck again, Megyn Kelly's show was cancelled in 2018, after a blackface incident, she left the network in January 2019.

MEGHAN MARKEL

Even Meghan Markel unfortunately falls within the category of Trump haters. She had clearly stated that she would never return to the US until Trump was out of office – within months, she was taking sanctuary back in California, USA after being slung out of Canada.

The president was not in her wedding guest list – to the very unconventional wedding services, in what looked like a carnival – but the press liked it – so my option was to switch over when my squirming got worse.

Her next hate move was not to attend the reception at Buckingham palace on the president's visit to the UK, which the media used to fan up the hate for the president and a foreboding retaliation from the president which caused such anxiety as we all wondered what was going to happen.

After the private audience with her majesty, we were all glued on to know how bad the situation had been as insinuated by the media.

Camilla, the Duchess of Cornwall's wink at the camera walking from the room gave us all such a reassurance that all was fine and to stop fretting. The talks with our Queen had gone well as she had re-assured us, much to the disappointment of Meghan Markel and the other Trump haters.

The Duke and Duchess of Sussex's rift with President Donald Trump escalated in March 2020 when Prince Harry was found to have accused the US president of having "blood on his hands" during a prank call with a Greta Thunberg impersonator. The president who has the greatest respect and regard for our Queen did not respond to that.

And then the hands of god struck – a British writer, Colin Campbell, 70, revealed that Prince Harry 'is less intelligent' than Meghan Markle and 'goes along with whatever she says' because he's 'desperate to please her' – that has not gone down well at all to the British public.

BUBBA WALLACE

In his attempts to gain notoriety, Bubba Wallace Jr. an American stock car racing driver decided to inform the media that someone had place a lynching noose in his garage. That news sends shivers down our spines all over the United Kingdom. That was most appalling in every letter of the reports – 'Lynch' and 'Noose'.

His father held several interviews and choked back tears when he claimed that his 'son had been having sleepless nights' and that the 'noose' incident was taking such a toll on his son.

As if the FBI did not have enough on their hands, fifteen were hurled in to investigate. The FBI determined that the loop of rope resembling a hangman's knot had been hanging as a garage door pull in Bubba's car for the past year, long before he was assigned the spot. Footage from earlier years showed similar garage door pulls being used by other drivers, although none can be described, exactly, as a 'noose.' It was not a hate crime.

Although unknown to many until the 'noose incidence', in April 2020, one of Wallace's sponsors had not taken too kindly to his continual flippant attitude and short fuse and decided to pull their sponsorship.

In the bid to improve his image, he opted to play the race card by wearing the 'Black Lives Matter' T-shirt in solidarity with protesters for justice in the death of 'George Floyd'. That did not quite pay off, so he delved further into politics and had gone on to campaign to ban the controversial Civil War-era Confederate flag at NASCAR events. That too did not do it, so further up he went with the 'noose' was meant to clench it – he had proved enough that he was anti-Trump and felt entitled to some attention to improve his image for sponsorship.

The driver faced a predictable 48 hours of bile and loathing across various platforms for race baiting, many wanted him to pay for the FBI's. In an interview on CNN, Wallace admitted that the backlash left him feeling frustrated and 'pissed'.

When the futile investigation was completed, the US president tweeted,

"Has @BubbaWallace apologized to all of those great NASCAR drivers & officials who came to his aid, stood by his side, & were willing to sacrifice everything for him, only to find out that the whole thing was just another HOAX? That & Flag decision has caused lowest ratings EVER!"

That was when I even knew who Bubba was. Not only had he wasted valuable financial resources, and created diversion from the pandemic and the protests in the US, the manpower could have been allocated somewhere else.

Bubba has gone significantly quiet; I could not find a peep before the book went into development. Also, hostility toward the racial uprising had begun, especially as the world realised that the death of Floyd George was used and exploited by Soros, the media Democrats of the BLM movement.

On July 4th, the paint had barely dried on the 165-foot long Black Lives Matter mural that was painted on the street when a man and a woman showed up and sprayed black paint on the yellow letters. It should be noted that even the New York City Mayor Bill de Blasio grabbed a roller a street mural.

De Blasio was flanked by his wife, Chirlane McCray, and the Rev. Al Sharpton as he helped paint the racial justice rallying cry in giant yellow letters on Fifth Avenue in front of Trump Tower.

BLACK LIVES MATTERS

Black Lives Matter is a movement that was formed in 2013, following the fatal shooting of 17-year old black boy, Trayvon Martin's, by Zimmerman, a member of the community watch, who had seen Trayvon behaving suspiciously, and had reported him to the Sanford Police. Soon after the call to the police, there was a scuffle and Zimmerman fatally shot Martin in the chest.

In June 2020, after the killing of George Floyd, #BlackLivesMatter soon morphed in the election year to turn violent day after day in major cities across the US with looting and arson.

Not only have the founders gotten into several illegal financial irregularities, they have also gotten into violation of IRS laws 501(c) (3) which prohibits the organization from engaging in campaign activity.

Even their purpose has changed, Patrisse Cullors, in her official capacity as a co-founder of the BLM Global Network, had told CNN that,

"Our goal is to get Trump out."

The movement has several donors which included George Soros. The members of the movement are enticed by the funding which enables the Democrats to stir up racial hatred, by paying the rioters to cause riots and chaos, destroy properties and loot stores, mainly in the black communities of Democrat run cities. The movement has profiled black people and shown by the mainstream media as disadvantaged low lives with nothing to do with the killing of George Floyd.

Early August saw the release of the police body cam footage of the incident. None of this conclusively exonerates the officers but highlighted several facts:

1. George Floyd was highly intoxicated and quite delirious and could not fully cooperate when he was being arrested. He said he was too claustrophobic to get in the police car and that he might die and couldn't breathe, even though he'd just been sitting in a car.
2. The officers were not aggressive and seemed to be communicating calmly to Mr Floyd.
3. George Floyd complained of breathlessness ever before he had a knee on his neck rather than breathlessness as a result of being knelt on.
4. The footage showed no racist comments all through.

The policies of the democrat run states include defunding the police, and,

"In fact, they just put out a pamphlet for citizens on how to be mugged without endangering yourself because they don't have a police force that can achieve anything anymore."

Another Black Lives Matter organizer Ariel Atkins defended the lootings and confirmed that looting was making up for the reparations that they did not receive.

7

EXPOSING WHERE THE BODIES ARE BURIED

Bottom line, the Democrats want the whole of America mirroring their Democrat run states – violence, defunded police, crime, run down rat infested with your jobs and industries outsourced to China. If they wanted it any different for the Americans, when they had decades to improve their Democrat run states, they could have done so.

It is all about using the people as political puns to take advantage of any crisis and they clearly stated, 'never let a serious crisis go to waste', and also demonstrated in the when Pelosi will not let the stimulus pass unless 'mail – in voting' is approved – which made the president to pass four executive orders to directly counter the hardship that she had wanted to impose on the people.

As soon as Trump decided to run for office, he began making comments that set off several questions in the minds of many American citizens and that the five main questions are:

- Why are all the Republican run states not as run down as the Democrat run states?
- Why are all the democrat politicians ostentatiously wealthy and their democrat run cities to derelict and run down with very high crime rates?
- Why is the president wrestling with the mainstream media and Democrats to gain the votes from the democrats run states to make them Republican?

- What has the president to gain when he does not need the black votes to win – he did not need it in the last elections and definitely does not need it now?
- Why is the president constantly engaging with community leaders of the Democrat run down states to directly target and fund policies to improve their communities and neighbourhoods?

The Democrats have the full backing of the media which they continue to use to block and distract the president from implementing his policies which are much needed to help the American people. Democrats want Trump out because the longer he stays in office, the more chances he would have to expose their corruptions and scandals which has enriched them – the sort of corruption you hear about in third world countries – if not worse – because of the amount of money and freedom from punishment with the aid of the mainstream media. The president has been pushed so hard that he is relentless in exposing them all – he knows where all the bodies are buried and he is taking both Democrats and mainstream media on simultaneously.

Despite their use of hoax news and their large broadcast capability the mainstream media are getting called almost every day on their fake news and their selective and obstructive method of interviewing. In leaving out factual issues, the president has seen to it that this is decreasing.

People are starting to question what they are being fed by the media and are starting to see that the media is becoming less factual all around, the truth is reaching the people, even the black American are openly speaking out on social media and asking why the Democrats have been in office for over thirty years and haven't done one thing for the betterment of black lives.

Quite simply, and especially during the former administration, it became obvious that the media just would not report on the greedy grasping practices of any democrats which would eventually get swept under the carpet and ultimately forgotten.

Most of these practices were right on the streets, in schools, hospitals, businesses and even in the White House itself, but no one was prepared or keen to talk about the obvious staring at their faces.

When Trump makes any accusations – the whole world runs for cover in shock panic and closer examination reveal that he would not have brought up anything new.

Trump has his tactics of calling out the politicians, he tends to bide his time until the offending politicians either expose themselves or provide Trump with the opportunity. Most of the time, they tend to expose themselves. We see this when Elijah Cummings strongly objected to Trump's border control policy Trump was quick to defend the border staff by calling out Elijah Cummings when he tweeted,

---

"Why is so much money sent to the Elijah Cummings district when it is considered the worst run and most dangerous anywhere in the United States. No human being would want to live there."

Cummings who died a few months later had received and pursed away $300,000 but the situation seemed to be getting worse. Apparently, in 2016, Bernie Sanders the failed democratic presidential candidate had tweeted that,

---

"Residents of Baltimore's poorest boroughs have life spans shorter than people living under dictatorship in North Korea. That is a disgrace.'

Even the mainstream media and the Democrats seemed to have forgotten Sanders' comments and went on full attack at the president. The attack suddenly ceased as soon as Sanders's comments were revealed. So what we have is Trump's strategy to expose and weaken the opposition in full glare of the media glare to maximum effect.

Then there is Hunter Biden, son of former vice president Joe Biden who took over 411 trips, which included trips to 29 countries, and five to China between 2009 and May 2014 and also took one and a half billion dollars $1,500,000,000 from the Chinese government, during former vice president Joe Biden's official 2013 trip to China.

With the election of his father as vice president, Hunter Biden launched businesses as a result of his father's power that led him to lucrative deals with governments and oligarchs around the world.

There was, for example, Hunter's involvement with an entity called Burnham

Financial Group, where his business partner Devon Archer who'd been at Yale with Hunter — sat on the board of directors. Burnham became the vehicle for a number of murky deals abroad, involving connected oligarchs in Kazakhstan and state-owned businesses in China.

Joe Biden's brother was not left out – he joined a company with no experience in construction – quite similar to the Burisma scam HillStone just as the firm was starting negotiations to win a massive contract in war-torn Iraq. Six months later, the firm announced a contract to build 100,000 homes. Hill Stone also received a $22 million US federal government contract to manage a construction project for the State Department, expected to generate $1.5 billion in revenues within the next three years.

Joe Biden, his father, having been exposed in 1987 as a plagiarist, also lied about his education and credentials and had 47 years to get things in order. If he could not do it in 47 years, many people have questions how he may achieve it in four years.

And then, there was Speaker Nancy Pelosi's husband. Before becoming Speaker, Nancy steered more than a billion dollars in subsidies to a light rail project that benefited a company run by a high-dollar Democratic donor and in which her husband is a major investor. She in fact owned the Goat Hill Plazer which was suspected of child trafficking and around February 11th.

Pelosi's husband is also a major investor in the company Salesforce which came under scrutiny for enriching failed presidential contender Tom Steye, she held a secret fund for Islamists and Hamas linked groups.

The corruption goes on, Pelosi's brother Franklin D. Roosevelt D'Alesandro was charged with lying during a rape trial in 1953 and a payoff kept him from getting charged with rape.

However, Trump's focus is on the underhand and rather villainous politicians; such as the pilfering mayor Ms Pugh who received

$500,000 for books meant for schools while on the board of the schools, Obama with a salary of $400,000 for eight years bought a property for over $15 million dollars in an estate called Martha's Vineyard which did not quite add up.

As far back as July 17, 2014 it was reported that the Company co-founded by Nancy Pelosi's son had two convicted criminals running the business and were all charged with securities fraud.

Paul Pelosi Jr., was the president and chief operating officer of Natural Blue Resources Inc., an investment company that focuses on 'environmentally-friendly' ventures. Pelosi owned over 10 million shares in the company.

The company was 'secretly controlled' by James E. Cohen and Joseph Corazzi, both of whom had previous fraud convictions. Corazzi violated federal securities laws and was barred from acting as an officer or director of a public company. Cohen was previously incarcerated for financial fraud.

I also noted that the hearing ended around January 15th, 2020, when Nancy Pelosi used the mainstream media to blank out the convictions by continually attacking Trump as being racist and xenophobic after he imposed travel restrictions on china.

Speaker Pelosi was also to hold the American's to ransom, by taking advantage of the COVID-19 pandemic to pursue climate policy and demanded things like new emission standards or tax credits for 'solar panels' – merely to prop up the family business while the American people were desperate.

I soon began to see posting on social media from rather uncomfortable democrat supporters commenting that if the party could hold the people to ransom and attack the president in that relentless manner and not working with him during the pandemic merely to protect their corrupt practices, there had to be payback time in November 2020.

US House Speaker Nancy Pelosi's son, Paul Pelosi Jr., 'was an executive of a gas industry company that did business in Ukraine' and was given a lucrative $180,000 a Year Position with Infogroup a provider of marketing services organisation a few weeks after his mother became speaker despite having no experience in IT or marketing.

Paul was also an executive at energy company Viscoil, a gas company. This job was directly because of Speaker Nancy Pelosi's influence because she was featured in the company's video advert to promote the company, he is also an executive of Viscoil's related company NRGLab, which did energy business in Ukraine. Paul Pelosi Jr. is also involved in various green corporate ventures that have not done so well and we all know that Speaker Pelosi needed the coronavirus stimulus fund for these ventures, instead of for the American people.

Other corruption included:

- Former DNC Chair Debbie Wasserman Schultz and her former aide Imran Awan were charged with bank fraud for wiring nearly $300,000 to Pakistan
- District Attorney Seth Williams, was questioned for not declaring $160,000 worth of gifts
- Congressman Robert Brady was investigated for bribing a primary challenger to drop out of the race in 2012
- Congressman Chaka Fattah was convicted for corruption charges. The Democratic congressman took an illegal $1 million loan to support his 2007 run for Philadelphia mayor, and then attempted to repay that loan in part with NASA grant funds. He further used $27,000 in charitable funds to help pay off his son's college loans and accepted an $18,000 bribe from a friend seeking help in becoming an ambassador, the report said. He was convicted in 2016 on 22 counts, including fraud, bribery and money laundering, and given a 10-year sentence
- Mayor Ed Murray was implicated in a sex abuse scandal
- The Democratic National Committee (DNC) is still embroiled in a class action lawsuit filed by Sen. Bernie Sanders supporters for rigging the primaries of 2016 in favour of Hillary Clinton. Another class action lawsuit by the Clinton campaign field organizers who weren't paid overtime
- Congresswoman Corinne Brown was convicted on several charges related to a fraudulent charity. Sen. Bob Menendez faced bribery charges
- Chicago Democratic Mayor Rahm Emanuel was faced with the scandal of the cover-up of police shooting unarmed black teenager Laquan McDonald in 2015
- Democrat backer John Coli Sr., was charged for extortion
- Democratic Gov. Andrew Cuomo's aides were charged with corruption and Cuomo diverted funds meant for Metropolitan Transportation Authority (MTA) repairs to boost his "pet projects."
- Democratic Congressman Anthony Weiner was charged for underage sexting
- And then there was Nader that faced numerous charges for sex crimes, as well as for helping a business associate funnel illegal campaign contributions to Democrats and the Clinton campaign in order to advance

- their political and business interests. He also served one year in prison in the Czech Republic in 2003 for molesting underage boys
- The Democratic Party and the media always focus on anti-Trump rhetoric but largely ignores the corruption among its members. The current Democrats in office serve as walking examples of why accountability is needed
- Kamala Harris had laughed off laughing smoking marijuana herself, but had criminalised and put thousands of people in jail for the same thing; which is not only a major hypocrisy and double standards, but also very dangerous for a politician in the position of power to practice a two-tier justice system
- As voters become privy to the party's incessant scandals, they become apathetic and of lately, encouraging the June 2020 rioting and anarchy that wreaked havoc all over the Democratic states
- Clinton approved the sale of 20% of US uranium reserves to the Russian company called Uranium One. She then received a multi-million dollar donation to the Clinton Foundation from Uranium One
- John Podesta, Hillary Clinton's campaign Chairman held $75,000 shares in Uranium One and claimed to have divested from it, but really transferred ownership to his daughter
- Uranium is an incredibly scarce resource used to make nuclear bombs, which is much depleted as Russia bought them in the deal brokered by Hillary Clinton and the Clinton foundation

DEMOCRAT AIMS

Although I follow Nancy Pelosi on Twitter, I still could not glean out a single positive that would benefit the people, all of which consist of absolute counter attacks on the president's policies; reader, take a peak yourself and scroll all the way down. The Democrats have been more successful in communicating aggressive attacks on the President than on their policies. The BBC and LBC helps them to drive their ploys, arguments and scams to ensure that Trump is not re-elected in November 2020. Their main focus is to ensure that the Democrats regain power by whatever means necessary and to prevent the President from exposing the Democrats' corrupt deals, and will go after literally any one that stands in their way – Trump Supporters –Trump's lifeline.

The Democrats know that many Americans rely on the mainstream media for their source of information and news on current affairs and would not bother to fact check or follow the events as they happen, hence all the people will get is the insistent attack on the president and every opportunity to advance their policies to suppress the people in order to gain their votes to subsequently facilitate lining their pockets, with policies such as;

Creating jobs for China and in China

- Outsourcing American Jobs to China
- Moving American manufacturing to China
- Investment mostly in China
- Infanticide
- Defunding the police
- Gun Control
- Riot and Violence
- Support for well-funded anarchists, thugs and looters.
- Illegal immigration
- Higher taxes of up to $4 Trillion from peoples' salaries
- Weak military
- Over regulation
- Let any one vote
- Welfare state – especially for the Black people
- Poverty and Suppression to encourage state Welfare
- Liberalism
- Communism

DEMOCRATS AND THE BLACK VOTES

The Democrats desperately need the black vote but they often take the black vote for granted by using the votes to amass wealth for the Democrats administration members and to suppress the black people even further to sustain the wealth of the Democrats.

The Democrats and the mainstream media continue to overlook the poverty and underinvest in the community. Until my research, I did not know about the rundown cities – I have heard about ghettos but mostly in movies, definitely not in the United States, until the president began to expose the problem and the causes.

The country has a plethora of historical landmarks, landscapes and homes, however several Democrat run cities are plagued with high crime rates, poverty, and unemployment.

Decades of corruption and greed in most of the Democrat run states especially Los Angeles, Chicago, Minnesota, New York has led to homelessness is a serious problem. Over half a million people go homeless on a single night in the United States. Approximately 65% are found in homeless shelters, and the other 35%

—just under 200,000—are found unsheltered on the open streets. Homelessness almost always involves people facing desperate situations and extreme hardship.

This has gone on for decades because the people continue to vote for the same Democrat policies that need them to remain in that state and keep them in that state.

President Trump did not wait until 2020, he began as early as 2017 to start direct investments in these communities and call out the Democrat run governors and mayors.

The president had exhaustively tried to highlight and inform the people that the rats infestations, homelessness on the streets, high crime rate, excessive food stamps, and high unemployment in most, if not all of the Democrats run cities was created deliberately for a reason – the black votes to keep the Democrats in office. During his campaigns, he asked the people in those rundown

Democrat run cities;

"What do you have to lose?"

Reader, the president really does not need to bother about the black votes, he did not need their votes and did not win the presidency from their votes, as attested by Hilary Clinton that argued that she had won the popular votes and the statistics. President Trump merely wants then included as part of the 'American dream', and to give back to the nation that had provided him with a lifetime wealth.

Trump's campaign promises include resolving the problems in those cities, but was continually met with strong resistance by the Democrats who have interests in the continual suppression of the citizens, majority of whom are from the black ethnic minority background.

Quite simply, it is in their interest to keep the black people suppressed in order to leave them dependent on welfare and the hand-outs serves to show that the Democrats cared for them so much and thus the need to vote for them during elections.

The coronavirus pandemic soon played into Trump's hand in exposing the extent of the corruption, from the continual blockage and delays of the coronavirus stimulus aid to the people by the Democrats.

The mayors and governors of the Democrat-run black neighbourhood promoted defunding the police, leaving the black people even more vulnerable to crime.

The rioting also played into Trump's hands as the people began to see the destruction of their homes, business and communities destroyed by BLM and Antifa. Most of his initiatives are blocked on one way or the other by the Democrats, however, the rioting provided the opportunity to speak with the black directly to confirm and provide what they needed to help the community, all of which were implemented without any obstructions from the Democrats – who would have rather left the communities in the rundown states up to November 2020.

Many people are now leaving these Democrat states, even in New York, companies are moving because of the Democrat policies of anarchy and destruction—even though the COVID crisis has waned. The rioting was but the last straw; New Yorkers were fed up with the shootings and lootings, homelessness on the streets, sub-par online schools, sky-high taxes and the sheer obliviousness, inattentive cares of the Mayor Bill de Blasio and Gov. Andrew Cuomo.

The Democrats may well preach socialism, however they have managed to amass wealth for themselves alone, facilitated from long terms of office which has resulted in corruption with impunity and until President Trump, many had looked on and accepted the situation:

Joe Biden—44 years in office
Chuck Schumer—39 years in office
Nancy Pelosi—33 years in office
Maxine Waters—29 years in office
Dianne Feinstein—28 years in office

All of which beggars the question of, if Pelosi was in office for all those years why are they trying to help the people only now. They are only there to simply to stop the president from exposing their corrupt practice, and as soon as they unseat the president, it will be even more difficult for the American to know about their corruption.

Donald Trump understands the importance of African American voters much better than Democrats and progressives do. Trump and his team are making sizable and smart investments in efforts to chip away at black support from the Democrats.

Reader, research on the riots. When BLM calls out for looting as reparation, those who want to oust Trump from the Oval Office are spraying millions of dollars in 'election spending' ONLY except in the African American communities to stop the rioting and looting. The most affected are the black citizens that put them there and in their calls to defund the police, law and order has ceased to exist in the Democrat cities and have been allowed to devolve into lawlessness with death and destruction, a myopic of how they want to transform the whole of the USA.

8

CORRUPT ILLEGAL DIRTY TACTICS

I have always regarded the FBI as principled law enforcement agents – almost like our MI5 finest, however, since Trump became president, he exposed some of what we all saw to be untrust-worthy, dubious and fallible.

The Democrats have never gotten over the fact that their candidate lost the 2016 elections to Donald Trump. From that day on, they have never stopped arguing that Russia handed the presidency to Donald Trump, and that the Russian interference effort started in 2014, when the Russians began planting the seeds of confusion in the United States election which had undermined Clinton's campaign.

The Obama administration had really been paranoid about Russia because Trump has a hotel and his business undertaking made them nervous that he may know one or two of their corrupt practices in Russia, so they began gathering intelligence on how to remove Trump by cooking up possible ways that Russia may be engaged in manipulating American politics.

However, the US intelligence community confirmed that there was interference, and although the Russian interference of spending thousands of dollars in social media adverts on hundreds of fake Facebook, Twitter and Instagram accounts was an assault on the US democracy, the impact was far too small to have any effect on the election; compared to the tens of millions spent by the Democrats on social media adverts for Clinton's campaign and the hundreds of campaign staff.

The meticulously mapped out plots were set up to hide the former administration's unethical – illegal practices and the longer Trump remained in office the likely their past illegal activities would be revealed and General Flynn was their weak link. He had worked with them, he saw all the goings on and was not playing along.

GENERAL FLYNN

The Democrats have claimed that Trump won the 2016 elections because of the sophisticated election interference effort; and that Russians promoted the Trump campaign and worked to disparage Hillary Clinton. Although the Democrats are now considering doing with the electoral college during presidential elections – merely because President Trump won the electoral college – this system of choosing a president has existed since Abraham Lincoln. When Americans go to the polls in presidential elections they are voting for the 538 officials who make up the Electoral College the group of officials.

The number of electors from each state is roughly in line with the size of its population.

Each elector represents one electoral vote, and a candidate needs to gain a majority of the votes – 270 or more – to win the presidency.

My friends and family, even those that live in the US never stop trying to convince me that winning the popular vote meant that Clinton won and that Trump simply declared himself the president, so when I say they frustrated me into writing this book, reader, you can now appreciate exactly what I mean. The democrats understand and know that the election was lost because Trump had won the electoral vote however, they continue to play on the people's ignorance by continually hoodwinking them into believing that the election was rigged because they won the popular vote. Trump's unexpected win meant the urgent need for dirty tactics to cover up, and their starting point had to be entrapping and accusing General Flynn.

The Democrats had based their accusations on an event that goes as far back as early 2014 when General Flynn had become a 'problem' for President Obama.

General Flynn had drafted a blueprint that confirmed the rise of a messianic mass movement of evil people, most of them in-spired by the totalitarian Radical Islam ideology, which revealed that Obama's anti-American national security policies had not only given rise to ISIS but had also allowed Iran and Russia to gain a greater foothold in Syria, Iraq, and across the Middle East – a formidable coalition. As a result of this revelation, Obama decided to stop communicating or consulting with Defence Intelligence Agency (DIA) Director Michael Flynn, the highest-ranking intelligence officer in the United States military. In April 2014, James Clapper, the then Director of National Intelligence forced out General Flynn from his post as Defence Intelligence Agency (DIA) Director. General Flynn also correctly predicted the rise of ISIS and exposed Obama's "wilful decision" to ship arms to the Islamic terrorists and of course, Obama did not want that information in the American public domain. The conspiracy was then hatched which involved Woolsey, Brennan, and Clapper – all senior CIA officials to take down Flynn and Trump.

In August of 2015, a whistle-blower Montgomery provided the FBI with 47 computer hard drives of illicitly-harvested surveillance data on domestic Americans which also confirmed that Brennan and Clapper illegally spied on Donald Trump and General Michael Flynn. This brought the Obama administration into a cold sweat because of the legal ramifications of spying on American citizens.

Woolsey then decided to frame General Flynn and despite Clapper firing General Flynn in 2014, hoping to keep their illegal acts would remain a secret. However, Flynn did come forward to expose the Obama administration's nefarious actions, in his book 'Field of Fight', Flynn exposed more very illegal actions by the Obama administration, but he also held back classified information that he could not reveal.

By February 2016, General Flynn began advising the Trump campaign and on November 17th, 2016, President-elect Trump named General Flynn to be White House national security adviser. Michael Thomas Flynn accepted Trump's offer for the position of National Security Advisor.

Although he was among the staff from the former administration, Trump believed in continuity and employee retention, a trait from his business background.

This appointment again aroused fear and confusion for the former administration and as such, they needed James Brien Comey, the Director of the FBI to act quickly on their behalf to remove Flynn. The American people simply did not have to know about the incompetent decisions such as the 'Benghazi affair' and more.

From as early as 2014, Obama and Hilary Clinton decided to have General Flynn spied on and this carried on to 2016 with the hope of finding sufficient information to either use against him and or even plant falsified information on him, he simply had to be removed.

In his diplomatic role, Flynn communicated with diplomats from various countries, including Russia that had peaked Obama and Clinton's suspicions and were certain to find something there to frame Flynn.

They then received confirmation that during one of these conversations, Flynn was reported to have talked with Kislyak, the Russian Ambassador to the US several months before during the Obama administration's new round of sanctions on Russia.

Despite the probe, members of the intelligence community confirmed with the response of 'nothing to see here'.

Meanwhile, the brand-new Trump administration was already developing close relationships with Russia and its president, Vladimir Putin.

In the first few days of Trump's administration, Russian Ambassador Sergey Kislyak and Michael Flynn got on the phone to continue to build that relationship via short, customary phone calls.

The conversation carried on normally to those in the room listening in as the two officials exchanged pleasantries and expressed optimism about working to broker a new era of US-Russia relations. But then, as the two officials were saying their goodbyes, Kislyak invited Flynn to the Russian embassy in Washington to eat Russian food. Flynn's response?

You keep telling me that."

That one, short phrase, to you and me meant – 'ugh! Russian food? No thank you'. However, Hilary and Obama decided to latch onto "You keep telling me that" of which the intelligence and national security staff in the listening room were warmly thanked.

FLYNN INDICTED

Flynn was indicted by Robert Swan Mueller, and the indictment stated that Flynn,

'Falsely stated that he did not ask the Russian ambassador to refrain from escalating the situation.'

That statement was in response to sanctions that the United States had imposed against Russia that same day.

Flynn had also told the FBI that he did not recall Kislyak subsequently telling him that 'Russia had chosen to moderate its response to those sanctions as a result of his request.'

That was how this 'dinner fly trap' was used during a casual conversation, and the FBI agents didn't tell Flynn that he was in fact was under investigation. In the next chapter, you will see how they adopted these same tactics with the president by Comey but failed.

FBI notes showed that bureau officials discussed that they had to interview Michael Flynn, who was just days into his new role in the new Trump administration in order 'to get him to lie'.

The notes of one of the questioning FBI agents was asking whether their goal was 'to get him (Flynn) to lie, so we can prosecute him or get him fired.'

This is frightening and it shows how easily one could fall foul of the FBI and how agents specifically schemed and planned with each other on how to prevent Flynn from knowing that he was in fact the person being investigated.

So they kept him relaxed and unguarded deliberately as part of their effort to set him up and frame him.

On December 1st, 2017, special counsel Robert Mueller agreed to a plea bargain in which Flynn pleaded guilty to "wilfully and knowingly" making "false, fictitious and fraudulent statements" to the FBI regarding conversations with the Russian ambassador.

Flynn's attorneys submitted a sentencing memo on December 11th, 2018, requesting leniency and suggesting that the FBI agents had tricked him into agreeing to make a statement during the White House interview and did not advise him that the statement would lead to him being indicted.

On February 13th, 2017, Flynn resigned as National Security Advisor, but three years on, in February 2020, after having destroyed his life, it was revealed that the FBI had since "lost" the original 302 summary report on the ambush interview with Flynn. Until Trump came along to expose and drain the swamp – who would have thought that of the FBI.

The FBI had 'pre-planned a deliberate attack' against Flynn, a decorated Veteran, he set up, plotted against and ruined just to make the Trump Administration look bad – you would think what chance the ordinary man in the street would have if the Democrats could do that to a 3-star lieutenant general with 4 Bronze Stars and the Defence Intelligence Agency director. In late April 2020, there was a flood of new documents about the "witch hunt" against the Trump campaign. Along with those reports were notes that Flynn had indeed been set up. Some documents appear to be exculpatory, meaning – they clear his name.

THE RUSSIAN INVESTIGATION HOAX

The Russian Hoax began when the FBI opened its official investigation on July 31st 2016. Trump's first term election rallies were furiously on, and the Democrats were confident that although very popular as a showman, the supporters only loved the personality but Trump could never be elected, most important of all, the Republicans had no alternative candidate. Notwithstanding, Trump had to be taken out of the process and this was to be an additional insurance even if he got through to becoming president by some 'hand of God'.

In fact, Trump had mentioned something out 'cleaning the swamp', during his campaign rallies and before he started expounding on that to his supporters, then the media, they needed a clear path to hide and continue with their corrupt illegal past deeds.

James Brien Comey Jr., the Director of the FBI was the central figure in the scheme to take Trump down, smear him with Russian "connections," through a hoax FBI "investigation" and more importantly, to trap him into a charge of criminal interference with the aim to distract and derail his campaign. There was no actual evidence of any collusion or connection between Trump and his campaign with Russia, but that did not prevent Comey Jr. from initiating an "investigation" at the FBI.

Comey's additional weaponry was to leak and drip feed news of the "Russia Investigation" to the main-steam media, who editorialised and exaggerated their versions accordingly and in the main, were continually egged on by the Democrats to keep the news rolling for as long as possible.

The shock of Trump's election victory spurred on the set up. Immediately after Trump was sworn in, both Hillary and Obama operatives and Comey began the direct attack – it was easier for them now, because the conspiracy had been in the public domain for a while now from trying to entrap Flynn. Not only that, for a while yet, the Department of justice (DOJ) was still controlled by Obama operatives also, initiating the investigation at the FBI had provided Comey (the Director of the FBI) with protection from Trump firing – it would be unthinkable to do that anyway – the TV personality would have the instinctive guts to do it – they thought.

Trump having foresight came into play. He may have known or had that hunch that being an ongoing investigation, he could not fire Comey, the implication being that if Trump fired Comey then it would be deemed to be that Trump was "interfering with the investigation" which in itself, is a federal crime that the FBI could then "investigate" toward an almighty scandal.

The plot from within was now set in motion and commenced with DOJ Obama appointee Sally Yates approaching the White House with news that innocent General Flynn had been in 'shady' contact with Russia and alleged that he might be compromised and emphasised that there was "additional information on the FBI investigation" into the allegations to present at the White House.

The second trap – a 'dinner fly trap' was a dinner invitation. The day before the promised additional information was to be sent to the White House, Comey set up a dinner with Trump. The trick was for Trump to ask Flynn anything about the investigation or Russia because any average person would use that opportunity to want to know or speak casually about the expected additional information coming from Comey the next day. The president fell for this trap – he loves his food.

The third trap simply had to work. To get Trump to question Comey about Flynn or try to get him to back off of Flynn or casually as in conversation how the "Russia" investigation was going on. This would have meant that the president was "interfering" and was bound to kick him out of office in a shot.

The fourth trap was for Comey to casually bring up Trump at the dinner, that several people involved with the Russians were being investigated but that Trump was not under investigation. Comey verbally directly steered Trump on two or more occasions during the dinner that he 'was not being investigated'. The menu selection must have been great because – the president was rather focussed on the meal and did not.

Watch this; in classic Trump foresight of knowing the impact of speaking out of hand to any Obama appointed official – an adversary and from his business background a major business competitor. Reader, can you now connect the essence of Strategic Competitive business experience and being light years ahead of understanding and reading people's body language, I do have the strongest belief that Trump knew it was a set up – ingenious scheme – but not when it is Trump being set up – Trump ignored Comey's nattering and carried on munching at his dinner.

An interesting point here is that Comey refused to mention the fourth trap publicly or when testifying in Congress – this would have convincingly proved that the conversations were being or that foreign intelligence gathering techniques were being used by Comey this too is a federal offence.

After the attempts to get Trump to comment on the investigation, both Sally Yates and Intelligence officials concluded and stated under oath that there had been no actual evidence of any collusion between the Trump campaign and Russia. You never attack Trump and expect 'the matter ended'.

Trump tells almost no one at the White House that he is about to play his hand. He always bides time and then lurches out his attack with such a fire storm – you do not know what hit you.

Trump gets both the Attorney General and the new Deputy Attorney General to legitimately review Comey's unprofessional actions at the dinner and it is recommended that Trump 'terminate Comey's employment with immediate effect'.

At this time, Comey was some 3000 miles away from the White House in California, and Trump prepared the dismissal letter with the recommendation from both the Deputy and the Attorney General. The dismissal letter went on to state that Comey had mentioned three times to Trump that he (Trump) 'was not under investigation'. The letter was hand delivered to the FBI headquarters by DOJ officials who have also been instructed to lock-down and seize everything in Comey's office, including all surveillance files ("tapes") of Trump and others. Comey's files, docs, computers and "tapes" were also taken to Attorney General Jeff Sessions' office at the DOJ, who has every right to have them.

On reviewing the tapes, Sessions discovered that Comey had surveillance tapes of Trump that contradicted what Comey had been saying to Trump. It is worth noting here that Trump ended up being disappointed with Jeff Session who was later to recuse himself from the probe because, being Trump's campaign adviser during the 2016 campaign he felt that because he (Sessions) had had meetings Sergei Kislyak, then Russia's ambassador to the US and although normal to communicate in the course of his role, Sessions had felt that recusing himself was the right thing.

Comey eventually got to learn that he had been fired when the media broadcasted it in California. He had no idea it was coming. Right on cue, the Democrats and mainstream media pack continued bellowing about Trump firing such a high-profile person as the director of the FBI because he was about to reveal that Trump was guilty of 'interference with the Russia investigation'. They did not know the correct reasons. The snippet leak that they were giving did not inform them about their own illegal plots – the main reasons for firing Comey and he left them to spill over their network for months. The great president had not finished, his next move was to tweet that,

---

"James Comey better hope that there are no "tapes" of our conversations before he starts leaking to the press."

This was Trump setting up the media to continue making their wild assumptions and discrediting. They bayed that Trump was "taping" everyone at the White House. However, only Comey and his cohorts understood the tweet message correctly the tapes were now safely lodged at the DOJ.

In effect, their plan had abysmally failed and the evidence was safely lodged at the Department of Justice.

The president's tweets made Comey capitulate. He told Congress that he will not testify and wrote a public letter to the FBI accepting his dismissal, stating that he did not want to discuss why or how he was terminated.

Trump hysteria and media frenzy had followed the news on May 9th, 2017 when it was reported that the president had fired James Comey, the seventh Director and the most senior official of the Federal Bureau of Investigation (FBI).

That was shocking. We all could not understand how the president could even contemplate doing that. A series of failed traps and scams had led to this sacking, but all that we knew at the time was that he was sacked for his handling of the FBI's investigation of the Hillary Clinton email controversy.

A statement was then issued to confirm that the "Russia Investigation" did not involve President Trump personally.

The democrats had again failed, they needed to hatch out another scam this would be the impeachment.

OBAMAGATE

Obamagate involves the unmasking of Michael Flynn. Unmasking is a routine operation in the US security service whereby US citizens liaise and interact with foreign persons to glean information. Usually, because of the nature of their roles, the citizen's identity is kept hidden, however, in order to understand the context of the information, sometimes U.S. officials can request that these hidden identities be "unmasked" that is, revealed.

What happened here was Obama directing the plot to unseat the incoming president.

This scandal involved twelve senior Obama officials including Joe Biden, Sally Yates – Former United States Attorney General, Lisa Page – Former FBI Lawyer and Susan Rice – Former National Security Advisor.

The real problem with this particular unmasking is;

● Eight days before Obama vacated the white house, which poses the question more of what did his administration have to hide that the 'unmasking' itself

- Secondly, it is very rare and unusual for the request to come from officials very high up
- It is also very rare to have this unmasking during the transition period, which ended up in the Washington post
- The impact of the unmasking had several implications;
- It allowed Obama to nullify and get rid of Flynn, the National security Adviser right away, leaving the new administration exposed not only the Trump administration but also the American people with no security
- It forced the incoming attorney general to recuse himself which left the new administration exposed with no Attorney General
- It allowed the new administration to be undermined continuously from within in the first three years and to cover up the truth
- The ultimate result of Obamagate was that it was intended to facilitate the Obama administration to continue and remain in office to keep power for themselves, but from the outside which we had continuously seen from the sabotage, leaks and false information to the media to attack the president
- Crucially, Trump had been voted and elected into office Obamagate was just not a criminal offence against the constitution but against every single American citizen – by setting up a coup to remove a duly elected president of the free world

Obama spied continuously on the Trump campaign and used the various hoaxes and investigations to stifle and distract the Trump administration for almost three years. They had wanted to continue to keep power for themselves and hopefully incapacitate Trump from exposing their corruption.

In the waning days of his administration, Obama conspired to entrap Trump's national security adviser, Michael Flynn, as part of a larger plot to bring down the incoming president.

The Justice Department released an inordinate amount of records that shed light on previously unknown Obama administration deliberations over Flynn, all confirming that Flynn had been illegally targeted and that the decision to investigate him went all the way up to Obama, the previous president.

President Donald Trump called for Obama who apparently had ordered Flynn to be spied on, to be interviewed before a congressional committee to formally explain his role in unmasking former National Security Advisor Michael Flynn.

Joe Biden's list, and comments from the attorney currently representing Flynn, links Obama to the crime "Obamagate" to target Flynn.

Obama and his staff used illegal spying powers to go after Trump leaving several incriminating trails of eavesdropping evidence – all of which we know are illegal.

Incriminating emails were also discovered as late as June 2020, also revealed illegal tactics by the former National Security Advisor and US Ambassador to the United Nations during Obama's administration, Susan Rice's.

The emails confirmed that Obama emphasised that Flynn be investigated,

---

"By the book, by the book, by the book."

Barely a week to the end of the Obama administration, instead of packing and emptying her locker on the new president Trump's inauguration day, she was sitting on her desk writing the incriminating emails. Even worse, she had previously lied that she knew nothing about the unmasking of Flynn.

Obama's and his senior staff members had abused their powers of unmasking to 'go after their political opponent', which was exactly what they had plotted and planted on president Trump in order to impeach him.

Obamagate is rather serious and it still remains to see how the president will get around this in time for the 2020 re-elections.

Although rather time consuming, the president has vowed a gloves-off re-election campaign that will include trying to discredit any and all potential general election opponents in order to pave the route back to the White House.

OPERATION CHOKE POINT

This was another illegal activity by Obama's Department of Justice (DOJ) who targeted small businesses for years, by using federal officials to pressurise banks to close the accounts of businesses solely because he was ideologically opposed to their existence.

Some government officials tried to deny the program's existence and it was run in secret until Trump brought it into the open.

The program, known as Operation Choke Point, operated unrestrained for years, with officials threatening banks with regulatory pressure if they did not close the business accounts of gun and ammunition dealers, payday lenders and other businesses operating legally, all of whom suddenly found banks terminating their accounts with little explanation aside from "regulatory pressure."

Apart from the secrecy, the problem with this controversial Obama-era program was hurting legitimate businesses. In a sweeping effort to push out businesses that the Obama administration deemed unsavoury in its eyes, its Justice Department used the banking system to force many small businesses out of operation. Some of these small businesses included gun sellers, small-dollar lenders, and other legal businesses the Obama administration disliked.

By targeting businesses because they aren't in line with the Democrat politics, what Obama did was illegal.

FAST AND FURIOUS

Fast and Furious was the 2009 operation involving the Bureau of Alcohol, Tobacco, Firearms and Explosives (ATF) which allowed the sale of thousands of semi-automatic firearms to criminals in Arizona who were affiliated to Mexican drug cartels.

The illegal acts came to light when several ATF officials turned whistle-blowers, to reveal that Obama had instructed gun store owners to break the law by selling firearms to suspected Arizona criminals. The ATF whistle-blowers were ordered not to intercept the smugglers but rather to let the guns "walk" across the US-Mexican border and into the hands of Mexican drug-trafficking organizations.

The political irony of this is that the Democrats kept on pushing for gun control in the media and to anyone that could listen, but in fact, those guns were later to resurface and traced deliberately to back up Obama's orations for political point scoring that, "...guns used in Mexican crimes mostly come from the US."

Several of these American guns were also used to kill Border security agents.

In effect Obama was committing criminal offences merely to improve his political position.

THE STEELE DOSSIER

The FBI's Russia investigation began in the summer of 2016 when investigators learned that a Trump campaign foreign policy aide, George Papadopoulos, had been approached by Russian intelligence operatives in London. They offered him "dirt" on Hillary Clinton and "off-the-record" meetings with Russian officials.

Counter-intelligence officers began to look into what was going on and by October, they were focusing on Carter Page, who had left the Trump campaign earlier in the year after he had served as a foreign policy aide.

In the new document from that month, the FBI not only argued that Page might have been conspiring with the Russians, it wrote that it believed he was a full-blown Russian agent. In the filing, investigators cited a number of reasons they believed it, including the FBI's past experience in dealing with Page — who had been targeted for recruitment by Russia's foreign intelligence service — and then, new reports the FBI was getting from a former British intelligence officer, Christopher Steele backed up their claims.

Steele was commissioned by a political intelligence firm, Fusion GPS, to investigate Trump's ties to Russia — a project that was being paid by Obama.

Steele's alleged 35-page report consisted of memos compiled before and after the November 8th election.

It included unverified claims that Trump let prostitutes perform 'perverted sexual acts' in the presidential suite of the Moscow Ritz Carlton Hotel.

Steele also falsified the document by adding that the President used the "extensive sexual services" of Russian prostitutes and that he attended "sex parties". In fact, the president slammed it as "fake news" because having done business in Russia he knows how rampart spying and surveillance is second nature to Russians and he even warns people of their spying nature often enough not to be aware of it himself,

"In those rooms you have cameras in the strangest places. You'd better be careful or you'll be watching yourself on nightly TV. I tell this to people all the time."

The material also suggested that Russia had launched a war of influence against the United States and that the Russian government had compromising material on Trump and Clinton that it could use to blackmail them — which has not been confirmed.

Many Republicans argued the DOJ and FBI officials appear to have deliberately concealed from the FISA judge that "Source 1" wasn't just someone with an axe to grind, but he seemed to have been paid to make those false statements. In fact, "Source 1" Steels lives in a country estate valued at £3.5 million.

Several people have also argued that the allegations in the dossier were not solid enough to merit being included in this request for surveillance.

House intelligence committee chairman Rep. Devin Nunes, also pointed out that the FBI knew that Steele had personal grudges against the president, which was not disclosed and as such the dossier was heavily biased.

Despite the president being innocent, the desperate Democrats still would not back down in their attempts to distract and deceive mainly the black people whom they are relying desperately for their November 2020 votes, and allowed the ranking Democrat on the House intelligence committee, Adam Schiff, to uphold that there was more evidence beyond the Steele reporting in the FISA application, but that he could not discuss the evidence because it remains a classified secret.

Few people know that the document was later released but this too did not detail much of the rest of the story, and entire sections of the file, including one under the heading "CLANDESTINE INTELLIGENCE ACTIVITIES OF THE RUSSIAN FEDERATION", were blacked out. Typically, to leave the people in their ignorant state, this point was not covered by the mainstream media.

FISA REPORT

The FISA Report – Foreign Intelligence Surveillance Act (FISA) oversees requests for surveillance warrants against foreign spies inside the United States by federal law. President Barack Obama had illegally arranged surveillance on Trump's phones at his Trump Tower office late in the 2016 presidential campaign and all of these were happening during the last months leading to the November 2016 elections merely to stifle Trump's campaigns and sway public opinion.

Members of the Obama administration's Department of Justice sought court warrants vias the FIA Act for the surveillance of Trump's former foreign-policy Mr Carter Page, allegedly for colluding with the Russian, but their warrant requests were based on a forged report funded in part by Hillary Clinton to smear Donald Trump during the current 2016 campaign.

The author of the dodgy report – named the Steele Dossier was Christopher Steele – a British former intelligence officer, had already been dropped as a reliable source by the FBI for leaking information to the press – that is typical Democrat strategy – sneak lies to the media who would blow it out of proportion, but the department of Justice continued with the surveillance, hoping to glean out any form of scandal to undermine president Trump.

Obama and his cabinet were literally staging a coup... fortunately they were incompetent and all their attempts failed abysmally.

THE HAMMER AND HILARY CLINTON'S DELETED EMAILS

Proof of Obama's indifference against ISIS came to the open, when a CIA contractor-turned-whistle-blower Dennis Montgomery's exposed John Brennan, former CIA Director, and James Clapper, former US Director of Intelligence during Obama's administration, of illegally commandeering a powerful surveillance tool known as 'The Hammer which should have been used for only foreign surveillance and not for domestic surveillance.

FBI Director Robert Mueller, who was later appointed Special Counsel for the Hoax Russia Collusion Investigation, supplied the FBI computers used to build the super surveillance system The Hammer, according to Dennis Montgomery, the computer expert who developed software programs that could breach secure computer systems and collect massive amounts of data.

On February 3rd, 2009, John Brennan and James Clapper illegally-commandeered The Hammer, and placed it inside a secret CIA facility in Fort Washington, Maryland, for unlawful 'domestic' surveillance, as exposed by whistle-blower Montgomery.

The Supercomputer "The Hammer" according to audio tapes has access to phone calls, emails and bank accounts of millions of ordinary Americans. The tapes also revealed that the Foreign Intelligence Surveillance Court (FISA), Supreme Courts Chief Justice John Roberts, 156 other judges3 that Russia had some incriminating information on Hillary Clinton that Russia could provide to the Trump campaign. He also stated that his source was from a Russian-connected Maltese Professor, Joseph Mifsud. Papadopoulos claimed Mifsud worked for the Russians and claimed that Mifsud had introduced him (Papadopoulos) to Putin's niece. On March 24, Papadopoulos decided to meet with Mifsud this time in London.

Papadopoulos said that Mifsud brought along with him a Russian woman, Olga Polonskaya, whom Mifsud falsely identified (he denied this later) as Putin's niece and that he (Mifsud) had information that the Russians have "dirt" on Hillary Clinton in the form of thousands of emails.

Papadopoulos also stated that he could facilitate a foreign policy meeting between candidate Trump and Russian President Vladimir Putin.

The man on the street will take these as an ambitious young man trying to make his mark up the ladder by impressing his superiors.

As it had happened, Clinton had used her private email from her private server for all her diplomatic messages. This was a serious breach of national security because it exposed the United States to foreign intelligence.

It then became public knowledge that Russia had hacked into the emails of the Democratic National Committee and of John Podesta's emails and Mifud's information was becoming plausible.

It then became public knowledge that Clinton had deleted thousands of her emails but further investigation still recovered more than 17,000 emails that had been deleted or otherwise not turned over to the State Department, and many of them were work-related.

On or about May 10th, 2016, at London's Kensington Wine Rooms, Papadopoulos allegedly told top Australian diplomat to the United Kingdom, Alexander Downer, that Russia was in possession of emails relating to Hillary Clinton.

The FBI dispatched a pair of agents to London on the secret mission coded 'Crossfire Hurricane' to meet the Australian ambassador, who had evidence that one of Donald J Trump's advisers knew in advance about Russian election meddling. After tense deliberations between Washington and Canberra, top Australian officials broke with diplomatic protocol and allowed the ambassador, Alexander Downer, to sit for an FBI interview to describe his meeting with the campaign adviser, George Papadopoulos.

Papadopoulos made at least six requests for Trump or representatives of his campaign to meet in Russia with Russian politicians, of which Trump's campaign chairman Paul Manafort forwarded one such request to his deputy Rick Gates, saying "We need someone to communicate that (Trump) is not doing these trips. It should be someone low-level in the campaign so as not to send any signal." Gates delegated the task to the campaign's correspondence coordinator, referring to him as "the person responding to all mail of non-importance." As such, Papadopoulos' information was not taken seriously and despite his communications with members of the Trump campaign regarding Russia, the Mueller Report found no evidence that Papadopoulos ever shared information with the Trump campaign regarding Russia having "dirt" on Hilary Clinton or possessing her hacked emails.

Meanwhile, the FBI decided not to charge Hilary Clinton, while they focussed extensively on the Russia investigation to unfairly undermine president Trump.

It is worth noting here that Paul Manafort and his deputy Rick Gates eventually fell prey to the controversy relating to the investigation. Manafort was handed a 43-month jail sentence but was released after 23 months to home confinement due to concerns about the spread of the coronavirus in federal prisons.

In a Watergate-level scandal largely ignored by the media, evidence continued to mount that the Obama administration was not only spying on President Donald Trump's campaign but was also fostering a resistance before he was even elected.

What happened next was another corrupt move. As soon as investigations started as to why she was using an unsecure method for highly classified messages, she set about deleting over 30,000 emails.

In effect, her actions breached security because she used the emails to send out classified information and that alone could have made it possible for hostile actors to gain access.

9

IMPEACHMENT FEVER

Around the end of June, my social media group chat account exploded with news about four rather unsavoury women, known as 'the squad', who got sworn into the Democrat House of Representatives and were soon to become the face of the Democratic Party at the 116th Congress.

Ilhan Omar who is best known for trivializing the 9/11 attacks, being unapologetic anti-Semitism and her bizarre personal life that features allegations of criminal and ethical violations as well as being investigated for a sham wedding with her blood brother, transferring more than $800,000 to her husband's company, Ayanna Pressley who is so uncouth and has the most venomous hate for the President and the police understandably, that intense dislike led her, as would anyone else with such abhorrence to lose all their hair,

---

"On the eve of the House's impeachment of President Donald Trump, the last bit of my hair finally fell out, and I have since spent some time experimenting with wigs to hide the loss, but the look didn't quite fit.

Ocasio-Cortez whose pitiful puerile comments on drives everyone distancing themselves with embarrassment, and the last of the four, Rashida Harbi Tlaib, unashamedly the most hostile and overtly hateful anti-Semitic and also a proud supporter of Islamic terrorist group al-Qaeda of the 9/11 attacks.

Rashida, the most uncultured of the four proudly showed her absolute disrespect for the President in the foulest of language, proudly commented "...let's Impeach the mother**cker already."

THE UKRAINIAN IMPEACHMENT HOAX

By early 2019, the stock market was scaling heights, manufacturing was coming back to the United States most important of all, unemployment had fallen to the lowest ever in forty years and crucially, the numbers of the ethnic minorities; Asian, Hispanic and African American saw very high employment numbers that had had risen dramatically and was continuing to rise to incredible heights.

Of course, the Democrats hated because it is customary for them to oppose and reject any positive impact on the American people. Which would be in direct conflict with their agenda – to disrupt, tank the economy and ultimately hurt the people.

None of the Democrats' false accusations and attacks on the president have ever managed to have any impact but continued to make for good entertainment as Trump supporters keenly post on social media on how the next scheme would end up in the Democrats being humiliated.

The impeachment was no exception. It was so obvious to all that the Democrats were faffing about, however the Democrats were desperate as elections were only ten months away.

Some of the Democrats and their supporters did not seem to understand the term or what the process involved, and they were ecstatic and jubilant that the president would be removed immediately after the Impeachment Trial by the end of January 2020. I was getting excited posts in all my social media timelines and after trying to explain to some twenty or so followers on a one to one and of course my friends and families, I simply gave up. At this stage, it was not the lies that were frustrating, but trying to explain how it would all end.

Put simply, impeachment involves a process of investigation and evidence finding that senior figures like judges, the president and cabinet members have to go through if they're suspected of committing offences while in office. In America, the political offence can include 'treason, bribery or other high crimes and misdemeanours.'

A vote will be taken as to whether the person has committed an impeachable offence and after it has been established they then go on trial in the Senate, the upper house of Congress – which was dominated by Republicans – the president's men – it was a forgone conclusion because Trump is very popular with them.

Many could clearly see that there was no basis for the impeachment and that it was a futile stunt in trying to be relevant in American politics.

What I found rather disquieting about this impeachment scam was the extraordinary part of US politics whereby anyone could concoct an obvious lie on an elected statesman, stitch up so tightly and get him to disprove the falsehood. That scariest bit was that they could do it with such impunity and without fear of being persecuted.

QUID PRO QUO

Impeachment — a posh word for indictment or accusation of a serious crime became the obsession for the Democrats as early as the first day of the president's inauguration centred on Biden and 'Quid pro quo', the Latin phrase that literally means 'something for something' or 'this for that.'

Right from the day of the inauguration, almost every comment from the Democrats revolved around impeachment.

In 2012, Ukraine was ranked amongst the top three most-corrupt nations of the world – alongside Colombia and Brazil. Corruption in Ukraine was deep and widespread, making it harder for both their citizens' survival, and for foreign investment.

Despite the IMF making accountability and transparency a condition of bailouts, Ukraine Foreign aid and investment funds simply disappeared with impunity into the banks of foreign individuals and Ukrainian citizens.

It was so bad that ordinary citizens had to pay a bribe for just about anything, even for basic transactions such as making dental or hospital appointments, getting a passport or driving licence.

The background to the impeachment started as far back as 2014 after a change of regime in Ukraine. When Hunter Biden, son of Joe Biden joined the board of Burisma, the corrupt riddled Ukrainian natural gas company. The appointment raised eyebrows because Hunter had no apparent qualifications for the job except that his father was the vice president in the Obama administration.

The Ukrainian natural-gas company that employed Joe Biden's son Hunter at $50,000 a month had also paid the former vice president $900,000 in lobbying fees.

Hunter Biden suddenly became a board director of Burisma despite having no previous experience in operations, or consultancy or if fact any work experience and that appointment seemed rather odd and fitted into the corrupt practices that the Ukrainians had alleged. Hunter Biden was also linked to multiple shady criminal activities involving fraud, money laundering and counterfeiting in Ukraine. Most concerning of all were the accusations that Hunter had established 'bank and financial accounts with Morgan Stanley bank, on behalf of Burisma Holdings Limited, for several money laundering schemes.

At the time, it was acknowledged that the Ukrainian corruption was far worse than the Democrats' and that the Ukraine prosecutor, General Viktor Shokin, who was ruthless at fighting the corruption of his country seemed to be doing a great job. However, Shokin soon became a controversial figure when his investigations began to creep closer to the corrupt US politicians.

Joe Biden was to openly offer his own 'quid quo pro' that president

---

," ...we had committed a billion dollars... Petro, you're not getting your billion dollars. It's OK, you can keep the (prosecutor) general. Just understand we're not paying if you do."

Trump was later to be falsely accused of, when he dangled $1 billion in loan guarantees as an incentive. Joe Biden had clearly stated

I would like to note here that Joe Biden did make the same 'quid pro quo', however, the media and Democrats feel that because it was Joe Biden, the offence mounted to nothing. In December 2015, Joe Biden pressured to force the resignation of Ukrainian Prosecutor General Viktor Shokin who was investigating corruption in Ukraine and– that was Quid Quo Pro – but Biden has never been called out on this.

On April 21st, 2019 the new President of Ukraine, President Volodymyr Zelensky was elected based on his anti-corruption ticket, and then three months later, a whistle-blower had assumed that a phone call in July 2019 between Trump and the Ukrainian President Volodymyr Zelensky could be an illegal 'quid quo pro' bribe whereby Trump would release aid as an inducement to having several 2020 presidential candidates investigated for corruption; the whistle blower also claimed that the gossip was rife among several White House officials and that officials had recorded and transcribed a word-for-word transcript of the call which confirmed his suspicions that the bribe was being offered.

The Democrats and the mainstream media decided that they felt that Ukrainian President Volodymyr Zelensky was a Victim and that Trump had 'threatened, and strong-armed him'. Confused at the suggestion, Zelensky continually stated that he was neither victimized nor blackmailed by Trump. Also, the transcript of the phone call confirms that it did not happen. The turpitude democrats then pushed the Russian collusion scheme for two and a half years and ended up with nothing.

The phone call that gave rise to the accusation came in July, when Trump tells Zelensky, in the words, 'I would like you to do us a favour'. Zelensky had won the election based on his anti-corruption agenda and many were claiming that American politicians fuelled the corruption. Trump needed to get to the bottom of the assertions and that included looking into business dealings of Hunter Biden, the son of former Vice President Joe Biden, and his business dealings with the Ukrainian natural gas company Burisma. The Wall Street Journal had reported that Hunter was being paid

$50,000 a month to serve on the board of Burisma, at the time that his father was serving as the Obama administration's point man for Ukraine. In Ukraine as in most developing nations having a Biden on the board conveyed the message of having sway with the Obama administration. That could influence events, including the course of investigations against the Obama investigations, without either Biden doing anything directly to cause it – in effect Hunter was the token bribe that was exchanged for the Ukraine officials' corruption.

The mainstream media would not report any corrupt deals made by the Democrats and the only way to have forced these to the public domain would have been for Joe Biden to appear as a witness. Joe Biden says he will refuse to testify voluntarily if impeachment trial reaches the Senate because he doesn't want to 'divert' attention from Donald Trump's 'crimes.'

Meanwhile, security and military aid of $391 million was being negotiated and was in the process of being transferred to Ukraine by the Trump administration. The issue here was whether Trump pressurised President Volodymyr Zelensky to investigate his 'political rivals before the transfer was made', with this, the idea of quid pro quo stood firmly at the base of the investigation. Another whistle-blower stated that Trump "is using the power of his office to solicit interference from a foreign country in the 2020 US election."

On September 24th 2019, House Speaker Nancy Pelosi took the extraordinary step of initiating impeachment proceedings against President Trump, accusing him based on the third-party hearsay gossip of violating the Constitution in seeking help from Ukraine to investigate Joe Biden. By the 19th of September, we learned that the investigation was actually about the presidential candidate's son Hunter Biden – of course – the Democrat's ignored this – they were desperate and the made-up hearsay gossip would be the best of their chances for an impeachment.

On December 5th 2019, Speaker Nancy Pelosi decided to declare that the House will begin drafting articles of impeachment against Trump, based on the futile malicious gossip the first step towards potentially removing the president from office.

The next step would be for a vote in the Senate House of Congress and a simple majority vote would decide whether to absolutely remove Trump from office. Although the Republicans held a majority at the Senate – they were hoping that at least five of Republicans may tip the scale, and if the vote failed at the Senate, Trump would not be impeached – 'accused' – and the process would end there.

On January 15th, as the world was experiencing the surge of the coronavirus spread, Nancy Pelosi and her Democrat cohorts were busy pushing for the president to be impeached – they did not care about the impact that the virus would have on the people, blinded with hateful sinister glint in their eyes, Nancy Pelosi handed out commemorative pens – with her name on them – after signing a resolution to transmit two articles of impeachment against President Trump to the Senate for trial and excitedly fixed a date for the Senate vote, for February 5th 2020.

Trump has repeatedly labelled the Ukraine call as "perfect", saying there was clearly no direct evidence of wrongdoing and the president also pointed out that Zelensky had reiterated that he never felt pressured. The Ukrainians were unaware the aid was held back for any reason, and eventually received it, after the necessary paperwork and transfer documentations were signed off.

COOKING UP AND COLLATING IN THE BASEMENT

The Democrats had sat in a basement for weeks conducting closed-door witness interviews and public hearings, and then strategizing on cooking and forging up the very weak case against the president that even non-legal observers could see through their desperate attempts. Most important of all, there was no chance that the president was going to be removed from office at the Senate which meant that they were merely desperately clutching on a careless word that could add to their allegations. At the time of the impeachment, there was a majority of 53 Republicans in the senate to 47 Democrats and the president had 96% or 99% approval from the Republicans.

Although the press would never report this, Trump is very popular among Republicans and members of the Electoral College. There was no chance of Trump losing this votes but again, the democrats relied on the press to continue their bawling of how unpopular the president was and how he was going to lose the impeachment votes – the sadness about all of these is that several people still literally believe the mainstream media and still get all their source of information from the mainstream media.

The impeachment which cost in excess of $1billion was based on conjectures and opinions of the event.

In effect, Trump was being impeached based on a basic scheme, hoping it would stick, this was part of the Democrat's attempts to stop Trump from exposing their corrupt practices.

The White House did not testify at Congress and there were several reasons for this:

- The invitation did not give the White House adequate time to prepare.
- The invitation did not provide information about the witnesses.
- The process has been unfair to him – the date of the hearing coincided to Trump's trip to London,

"Scheduling the hearing 'no doubt purposefully' to conflict with Mr Trump's visit this week to London for a Nato summit. He is due to return to Washington after the judiciary committee hearing."

After having spent fourteen days in a basement desperately trying to hatch out anything that might lead to an impeachment, the Democrats still could find no prima facie case based on the hearsay evidence of the whistle-blower.

The Democrats knew all along that the obstruction of justice sham was based on a phone call that was not compelling, the abuse of power charge was not evident from the phone transcript, which was made up of second and third-hand hearsay – however, disruption fitted into their agenda, they Democrats decided to make up a case and so they went along with the impeachment. They had failed dismally in their coup.

Firstly, the President was falsely accused of seeking help from Ukraine's government to get his second term re-elected by dangling millions of dollars of military aid and a White House invitation meeting at Ukraine's president if he investigated Joe Biden, the transcript of the phone call did not show this and the Democrats could not come up with any evidence to back up their conjectures.

Secondly, 'hearsay' witnesses assumed that Trump had abused his power by pressuring Ukraine to investigate former Vice President Joe Biden, the man likely to challenge him – at the time of writing.

From as far back as 2018, various news feeds have concluded that Mr Biden would lose to Trump if chosen as the Democratic candidate or may even be declared suffering from dementia and the appointed vice will be spirited to take over as the one to contest with Trump. As early as January 17th 2020, following the China ban, I had in fact posted that I am the first to congratulate president Trump for the November 2020 elections.

Thirdly, the desperate Democrats knew that although the witness accusations were weak, even I know that it is illegal to ask foreign entities for help in winning a US election – depending on the responses to the allegations, the Democrats were hoping that from people testifying, the most microscopic word out of place may help with their conjectures.

Fourth, and most crucial to the impeachment was that the whistle-blower did not directly hear the conversations at all between President Trump and Ukrainian President Zelensky. Rather, over six White House officials had carried over the Chinese whispers which eventually reached the whistle blower and he then assumed that it could be used as an impeachment evidence. Many contributors to the various group chats have claimed that the whistle blower had been paid to take on the mantle, with the guarantee of protection from being revealed as is usually the case for whistle-blowers.

SCHIFF'S HOAX OPENING STATEMENT

The president and his formidable legal teams, headed by Jim Jordan waged an incredible campaign to discredit the whistle-blower and based their key argument on the fact that it was obvious that the whistle-blower did not have first-hand knowledge of the situation – it was all based on gossip from third parties.

The whistle-blower was not going to testify and at this, many were certain that the whistle blower did not even exist and that the impeachment was a desperate made up lie to distract the president, distract the nation and make the people suffer.

The week before the hearing the president decided to play his hand – he tweeted for all to pray for him. That message even rattled me. I quickly posted an interceding prayer to Our Lady of Muswell, who never fails to turn curses into blessings. Many others had posted various prayers as well.

On September 26th 2019, under oath, Schiff gave his own spin on the opening presentation. The first two minutes of the hearing was a bare faced lie – even admitted by Adam Schiff himself.

It started with the House Intelligence Committee Adam Schiff who made himself a fact witness, lead investigator, accuser and judge.

The debacle of the impeachment soon backfired from the very start when Schiff delivered an ill-advised parody of Trump's July phone call with President Volodymyr Zelensky of Ukraine. Schiff had been under oath and that 'jest' made it detrimental to the Democrats because they lost a huge number of their support base who had just switched on only to hear a conjecture.

Trump's defence lawyers, headed by the redoubtable Jim Jordan accused him of misstating the evidence against the president and running an unfair investigation. Apparently, he too did not participate in the closed-door depositions conducted by the House intelligence committee and the President was denied the right to cross-examine witnesses who would have had to include the elusive whistle blower that was protected from being disclosed and other Democrats; including Speaker Pelosi that had corruptly amassed millions of dollars from several deals in Ukraine.

Schiff had concocted in the opening statement that Trump had asked Zelensky, the president of Ukraine to 'make up' or 'manufacture' dirt on former

Vice President Joe Biden. No one had heard that, not even the mainstream media.

After the unanimous outcry that his opening statement was false, Schiff went on to state that his made-up accusations was 'the essence of what the president communicates' in his call with Zelensky.

When Jim Jordan, pointed out the embellishment, Schiff mischievously grinned at the camera stating that his lie was a 'harmless joke' and went on to explain to the rather bemused world glued to their set on the different world time zones which sentences were his own comedy sketch and which words related to Trump's comments.

As expected, the comedic "parody" backfired. The desperate Democrats could not believe what they had just heard.

The three week 'popcorn event of the year' ended in five minutes as the impeachment debacle lost momentum and interest. The Democrats should have given it all up by now – however – in order to save face – the Democrats thought it best to carry on with their embarrassing façade and eventually got round to taking their votes to set a date to take the acquittal or impeachment vote to senate. The date was set for January 22nd 2020.

RESULTS AND IMPACT OF THE IMPEACHMENT

On February 9th 2020, while the novate coronavirus was ravishing the world, the Democrats continued distracting it from us with their hoax impeachment.

The Senate, of 52 of the president's fellow Republicans, voted to acquit him against 48 democrats on charges of abuse of power and 53 of his fellow Republicans and 47 Democrats on obstruction of Congress.

Mitt Romney was the sole Republican to vote to convict the President on the first article of impeachment, 'abuse of power', however, he joined with the Senate, run by the president's fellow Republicans and voted to acquit him on the 52-48 not guilty vote.

In the end, Trump was cleared of abuse of power and obstruction of justice and the Senate voted in favour of acquitting President Trump in the impeachment trial. The impeachment was doomed to fail from the start, all that was intended was to put a stain on the president's records. On the face of it, President Trump had been totally vindicated the whole debacle enraged and energised supporters on social media and they all sought vengeance for the spate of wilful spite and hate hurled at Trump, which will be on November 3rd.

President Trump was found not guilty in his impeachment trial, which ended the bid to remove him from office that had bitterly divided the US but had begun to unite the nation as many, including the Democrat supporters could see the game being played by the Democrats.

Mr Trump, always protested no wrongdoing. And his re-election campaign released a statement that,

---

President Trump has been totally vindicated and it's now time to get back to the business of the American people.

"The do-nothing Democrats know they can't beat him, so they had to impeach him. This terrible ordeal was merely a Democratic campaign tactic."

Republican Senator Lindsey Graham, concluded in his statement that,

---

"We have been working on this for the past 2 and a half years."

This meant that the so-called crime which they claimed took place in June 2019 was being schemed thirty months before it even happened as far back as 2016.

While Democrats were diverting the attention and energy of the entire country into a pointless trial that could not possibly have ended in anything other than President Donald Trump's acquittal, the coronavirus pandemic that was raging through China and had landed in the United States.

The impeachment debacle can be summarised in the following:

- 22 months
- $30 million

- 19 lawyers
- 40 FBI agents
- 500 witnesses
- 2800 subpoenas

To tell us all what we already knew – No collusion. No obstruction.

10

TRUMP SUPPORTERS

"To the people who fly private but lecture us about the environment. To the people who live in gated communities but lecture us about building walls. To the people who travel with armed guards and lecture us about guns, your bottomless hypocrisy is why America choses Trump." – Candace Owens

The president's support base is made up of three main classes;

- Those that simply love his humorous personality
- Those that only like his policies
- Those that love both his policies and personality
- Those that simply need a change in their dismal life

I beggar to see any opponent with one or a combination of the above. Most of the president's supporters have commented that the president is not a career politician and that if they wanted a perfect person, they would have elected a Roman Catholic monk they voted for a person that they believed can and would get the job done – and he is performing accordingly as promised.

DEMOCRATS FOR TRUMP

TRUMP 2020 launched the 'Democrats for Trump' coalition on December 19th, 2019. This ingenious master stroke is aimed at attracting disaffected Democrats who will refuse to support witch hunts, sham impeachments, or radical big government socialist policies and speaks for a generation of Democrats who feel abandoned by today's partisan tactics and may soon lead to the democratic solution of checks and balances.

Nearly two-thirds of voters in six battleground states who voted for President Trump in 2016 say they intend to back the president according to polls by The New York Times Upshot Siena College in November 2019. Some supporters have stated why they voted for Trump in 2016 and will again in 2020,

"In the last couple years, the Democrats had kind of been losing the work, and I thought Trump might get us that work, and to be honest, I've been in construction 21 years and the last two years were the best years I've ever had."

"I've been a Southern Democrat all my life, but in 2016, I cast my first Republican vote because I like that Mr. Trump is a businessman, not a politician — and I dislike Hillary Clinton."

"If you're going to Washington, you need to do something, If the only thing you're going to do the whole time you're there is try to get rid of the president, that's a problem. I mean, Trump is not a great person, but you've got to get some work done."

In the survey, 7% of those who supported Mrs Clinton in 2016 said they now approved of the president's performance despite his personality and his Twitter account.

"He's not exactly the person I'd have as my best friend, but he's a great president. Most politicians just talk about doing things, but Trump does them."

Late 2016 began to see the start of Trump derangement syndrome, the sickening hate from the Democrats and their supporters. 2020 saw a different type of abhorrence and detestation.

One Denver city councilwoman Candi CdeBaca cheered on a message about spreading the coronavirus at one of President Trump's rallies when she tweeted,

"For the record, if I do get the coronavirus, I'm attending every MAGA rally I can."

Radio celebrity Howard Stern has always been anti-trump, but in April decided to go for the Trump base supports by inviting them 'to all drink clorox and drop dead.'

Many of the voters cited economic strength as a major reason to support Mr Trump in 2020, even if they didn't support him last time. Also, certain voters who support Trump said they had soured on Democrats because of partisan fighting, culminating in the ridiculous impeachment hearings.

"The wheels are turning in the right motion for a lot of people who it wasn't for the longest time."

This survey was in December 2019 before COVID-19 lockdowns, which has greatly impacted the president's two winning trump cards.

"The Democratic Party fell apart on the heels of Trump winning, the harder they're going after Trump, the more they're just alienating people and pushing them away."

"Mr. Trump is 'an egotistical, overbearing man, but said that doesn't change what he's achieved."

Interestingly, Trump supporters' group chats have many people posting jokes. The supporters just love to laugh – amazingly, you can almost tell a Democrat by the look of their bitter and twisted faces.

BLACK ETHNIC MINORITIES FOR TRUMP

Nothing could be more intimidating and unnerving to the American Democrats and the mainstream media than ethnic minority Americans who think for themselves. Black people who question Democratic policies, from social programs to public education, are so vehemently demeaned by other black people. You see this on most African American group chats as well as on other right-leaning groups and broadcasts such Mark Kaye, Wayne Dupree, David J Harris Jr, An Omaly and Dan Bongino, without whom I could never have found invaluable material related to what was being left out by the mainstream media.

African American voters are staggeringly Democrats, and as such, without them, there would be no Democratic Party. So, when these Black people begin to question the damage that the benefits and welfare state that is being done to black people or the education systems that trap minorities, the censures are even worse for Trump supporting black people. On social media a black US Comedian Steve Harvey was eviscerated for accepting an invitation to meet with President Trump, although he had openly supported Hillary Clinton in the 2016 election. The black columnist Cynthia Tucker was to say that, "He will likely be remembered as the GOP's latest black mascot, a court jester, a minstrel show."

Despite being labelled a racist, the president also has many high-profile black supporters such as Candace Owens, Diamond and Silk duo, the Hodge Twins and the greatest of all black Trump supporter Terrence K Williams – the one most likely to take the proverbial bullet for Trump.

The president's support does not end in America, it extends all the way in Nigeria. As early as April 2017, I began to notice on social media that there were quite a few die-hard supporters all the way in Nigeria. Facebook accounts of the likes of Ike Chikudulue and Emeka Mbanefo are fighting his corner as far as the Nigerian followers are concerned.

With accolades such as;

"Trump Odogwu (Trump the greatest of the greatest)"

"Trump Okwu Eme (Trump- Promises made, Promises kept)"

"Trump Chineke diri gi mma. Idi ike na enu ike."

"Chideraa Odego!"

"Trumpgidigbam Gidigbam!!!"

All of which are very high accolades of privilege granted as a special honour or as an acknowledgement of merit granted to senior traditional ruling chiefs in the South-Eastern region of Nigeria.

When Trump was proclaimed the first 'black' American president there was every bit of truth to that.

It was around this same period that many Americans were beginning to see an immediate impact in their pay packets as a result of the tax reductions which saw many noticed that their pay cheques had on average gone up by 15%. In addition, many long-term unemployables were beginning to get work. President Trump did not need the black votes to win – in 2016, and the few that may have voted for him was quite negligible.

That direct strategy of working for the black people as early as 2017 and not as late as October 2020 has worked for the black ethnic minority in America whom Trump had asked in August 2016 when he sought the African-American votes, "...what have you got to lose."

It has completely paid off for those that voted for him as well as for those that did not.

The African-American segment was beset by crime and gun violence, higher unemployment among black men within ages 17-34, higher incarceration rates and second-class schools and second-class teachers. By the end of 2019, barely three years in office,

Trump was later to pardon several nonviolent prisoners who had been incarcerated by Joe Biden. As pride in being employed sent the focus away from crime and gun violence, while the Democrats with the aid of the media continued beating their incessant drum of propaganda about President Trump being a racist – they fear that black people may begin to appreciate that Trump's promises are not campaign gimmicks.

Candace Owens, the conservative commentator and political activist was relentless on her videos which stated that, "The minorities especially black Americans had been sold the 'Democrats victim chapters' for a long time, and they were doing a 'Blexit' – coined from our British 'Brexit."

Candace's Blexit ('Black and exit') movement which was launched in 2018 aims to encourage African-Americans to abandon the Democratic Party and register as Republicans.

Many Democrats are beginning to realise that black people are now proudly openly supporting the president because of his policies that have directly impacted them, and are clearly becoming the lynch pin and core to his support base in the swing states.

As the Democrat impeachment scam began to sprout, many social media posts from the black supporters were happy with the feel-good factor that they experienced from working.

Many had stated that they were convinced that the Democrat's constant assaults on the president were not only because they lost and could not move on but because he was likely to expose something; corruption, diversion of funds to personal accounts etc which translated to the run-down state of their communities.

Quite simply, corruption is rife in most of the Democrat-run cities as seen in the destitute state of their communities, the homelessness, and crime. Despite the lavish lifestyles and the inordinate levels of corruption of the politicians of the cities ran by the democrats, the black people will tend to trust and follow a black politician more – and as such turn a blind eye to the fact that their terms of office are inordinately long and that most of them have the job for life or die on the job in their community that they call home.

It all boils down to the trust of being of the same colour and it has been like that for decades, but then came Trump. When Trump had said, "...look at your condition for decades, just this once... What do you have to lose", was now beginning to make sense to many.

A black vote for the Republicans poses an absolute threat to the Democrats' styles and a black Democrat vote serves mainly to keep their suppressors in their lavish lifestyles with funds that are meant to go into the communities' swells.

The Director of Americans for Prosperity, a non-profit organisation Demetrius Minor went on to write that,

"Black conservatives are targeted because they defy the status quo and ignore the stereotypical imagery of blacks being one-dimensional and not having an open mind."

He did not go further to analyse the implications and reasons: corruption and post for life.

More black people are agreeing and confirming that Trump is positively responsive to their needs. He may be accused of pandering for the ethnic minorities' votes, but many online commentators have rightly stated that the president did not win the 2016 elections from the black votes, and since he came into office until the pandemic, they had seen their employment numbers and earning increase. Many appreciated him because their standard of living had dramatically improved. Although many would not openly admit enjoying the benefits.

The black numbers in support for this great president soon became obvious on social media and at Trump Rallies of all places and by March 3rd 2020, the last rally at rally in Charlotte, just before the coronavirus lock down, there was a good sprinkling of black faces, with proud black men and women of all ages partaking in pre rally interviews with the Right Side Broadcasting Network (RSBN), among the extensive queue of thousands of Trump supporters waiting to get into the arena.

"One of the most threatening places to be in politics is a black conservative," commented Senator Tim Scott at the sight of 'Blacks for Trumps' in the rally.

If only they knew that their hate was awakening the silent dormant voters that are fed up and frustrated about the inordinate hate being spewed out every hour from both US and UK mainstream media. The hypocrisy of it all is that the democrats are all about hate for stereotypes yet encourage the stereotype that says black people have to support the Democrats in the USA. The problem now for the Democrats is that more black people now confirm that Trump is positively responsive to their needs and are now openly admitting enjoying the benefits of his targeted policies.

DIRECTLY SUPPORTING THE BLACK COMMUNITY

Hoping to steer the black communities away from the divisive mainstream media as seen, following the June 2020 riots, which the media, with their ferocious feeding frenzy had fanned the Democrat's vicious attacks into being a 'race riot', the president held a listening session with some people who wanted to be heard about the needs of the black community.

During the session, the participants identified four major issues they believe were critical priorities for the black community that may help to pacify some moderates. The four priorities that were identified included very visible:

1. Economic Development
    - Which would eliminate many of the financial and regulatory barriers to starting a business in the inner city, particularly as many were having to rebuild after the rioters had burned down or otherwise destroyed their facilities. Through the Minority Business Development Agency (MBDA), the @realDonaldTrump Administration has helped facilitate billions of dollars in funding to support minority enterprises.

2. Confronting Health Care Disparities
    - Obamacare had failed many and they needed focus on the personal health habits of black people. Obamacare health care relies heavily on employer-provided insurance, and they needed to access their own care.

3. Professional Standards in Policing
    - Everyone recognized that the death of George Floyd was totally unethical and they needed the police to review their policies and procedures a priority which was of particular interest to President Trump.

4. Mental Health
    - The president has already seen that programs are in place that would see social workers join with police officers to explore approaches to problems, since mental health seemed to be the reason for a high number of crimes and in fact in not only the Black community. Even if the Democrats went to the deepest of Agenebode in Nigeria to get a black woman for vice president – there will be no stopping the great president Trump.

The choice is simple. There is no other choice.

WOMEN FOR TRUMP

Many unprecedented numbers of women supporters have attested that despite media barrages on the controversial misogyny accusations, they will vote for him again in 2020.

Many became supporters merely because of the media hysteria on the false and unfounded accusations – proven by the various social media groups and websites for women that support the president and empowers women to proudly vote to re-elect President Trump. On Facebook, 'Women for Donald Trump' boasts 78,000 followers while 'Real Women Vote Trump' boasts 222,000.

At the time of writing, I could not find women group followers on social media for Joe Biden.

The number of women supporters has since grown with several commenting that there are more important issues than the president's remarks.

Many have applauded the way he has hired women, who make up over half of his staff, notably political consultant Kellyanne Conway, and of lately, the formidable Press Secretary Kayleigh McEnany for very high-profile roles and that they are such a match and perfect fit for their roles.

According to the Pew Research Centre, women tend to vote at higher rates than men. And numerous studies of voters in key swing states, like Pennsylvania, Michigan, and Wisconsin, have found that white working-class women could determine the next president.

MOSLEMS FOR TRUMP

Republicans account for a small but steady share of US Muslims. Some groupings of US Muslims identify with or lean Republican but many more US Muslims identify with or lean toward the Democratic Party than the GOP (66% vs 13%), but the share who are Republican has held steady over the last ten years, including after the election of President Donald Trump, according to a new analysis of Pew Research Centre survey data collected between 2007 and 2017.

Muslim Republicans are much more likely than Muslim Democrats (45% vs. 11%) to say immigrants are a burden to society because they take jobs, housing and healthcare, according to a survey conducted by the Centre between January and May 2017.

As might be expected, Republican Muslims are less likely than Democrats to see the Republican Party generally, and President Trump specifically, as unfriendly toward Muslim Americans.

In support of the Muslims, Donald Trump's envoy Sam Brown- back decried China's 'war on faith' as President Trump hosted survivors of religious persecution from seventeen countries and US Ambassador-at-Large for International Religious Freedom.

Sam Brownback, Donald Trump's ambassador-at-large for international religious freedom has since emerged as the face of America's support for Muslims in China and Myanmar, to the surprise and elation of most of his earlier critics, for defending the Uighurs Muslims detained in what he referred to as "concentration-type camps" in China.

LATINOS FOR TRUMP

Millions of Latinos are Trump supporters. In the 2020 election, Trump seems likely to get between 25%-30% of the Latino vote. A recent poll by Telemundo found that 1 in 4 American Latinos would vote to re-elect him.

In 2016, according to exit polls, Trump got 28% of the Latino vote. Anything above 30% is a decent showing for a Republican, and anything beyond 40% will make a GOP candidate virtually unbeatable.

Latino voters count for a lot. Three reasons: they're a young population that is adding new voters at a staggering rate; they are well-represented in so-called battleground states such as Colorado, Nevada and Florida; and close to two-thirds of Latinos are Mexicans or Mexican-Americans, who tend to be swing voters.

Latinos are now poised to be the largest racial or ethnic minority group to be eligible to vote in a presidential election, according to the Pew Research Centre. By 2020, an estimated 32 million Latinos will be eligible to vote, which is just slightly more than the 30 million voters who are African-Americans. According to Pew, Latinos are expected to be about 13.3% of the electorate in 2020.

Blacks for Trump, Jews for Trump, it just goes on for President Trump. Most of these groups have one thing in common, they all value his policies over anything else. They have all directly experienced the impact of his policies, especially the policies linked to the economy, the health of their local economies especially before the pandemic, building booms, more jobs, and more people out shopping.

The other big factor for his supporters are what they call his "respect" for them, unlike Hillary Clinton's remarks about his supporters being 'deplorables'.

TRUMP RALLIES FOR SUPPORTERS

There was a time when the BBC news could be relied upon to provide factual reporting but not anymore. Like me, many may be forgiven for not knowing about Trump until soon after he became president and could be pardoned for not knowing about Trump during his campaigns... fast forward to 2019 / 2020, none of his amazing rallies were aired on UK television.

Many have turned to direct news feed sources with the aim of processing the information themselves. The direct news feed is still not enough, and many seek the un-edited live speeches without any form of media intervention or editorials, the live rallies are a really good source of getting the president's direct and unadulterated words.

The rallies are so popular that as soon as the president announced his first post-coronavirus rally in Tulsa at an indoor sports and events arena that has more than 19,000 seats – there were over 800,000 tickets demanded – the Democrats were not happy and were soon to put their usual degenerate scheme in place.

A typical Trump rally follows the same supporter experience. Trump is entertaining and as the events attract incredible media coverage, he uses it to the maximum advantage:

- Announcing new policies,
- Repeating his achievements over the past years,
- Highlighting the flaws of the opposition,
- Correcting the latest Fake News
- Emphasising Fake News that have backfired

- You will have to learn to write and speak Chinese
- China and Iran are hoping Trump gets defeated
- Trump has been tougher of Russia than Obama
- Trump wiped out ISIS

The supporters came from all walks of life and ethnic backgrounds but all united behind one purpose – We Love Trump. There is community at a Trump Rally – a day out with fellow Americans that share the same interest – Trump.

Quite unlike being sat behind a computer, 'following', 'liking', 'sharing' or 're-tweeting', here you are met with real followers from all walks of life, all united behind the American flag.

On arrival at the area, supporters are met by a Secret Service blockade. The staging area is roped off to form an orderly meandering queue for the 30,000 odd supporters who already expect a six hour wait. Most if not all are decked up in Trump regalia and there with even more trump MAGA and KAGA clothing, T-shirts and Caps for sale. What is key is the friendliness and unity of the various races and backgrounds – a microcosm of what an ideal American living in harmony could be like.

The cold weather does not deter them, they were all excited to be there, it is more like a music festival experience, and you could always almost spot the regular Trump rally fans with their relaxed look and slightly worn apparels unlike the novices that came prepared with folding chairs, food coolers hampers, drinks packets of snacks food.

The queues are not static, every five minutes, supporters would pick up their chairs, food drink coolers, and other paraphernalia to move forward about six feet, then hold for a few minutes and repeat the process as they snaked towards the auditorium.

Some twenty yards toward the entrance, the snake would branch out to four or five lines towards the steps of the arena entrance, to go through security.

The armature Trump rally supporters would learn that food, drinks, vapes, lighters, packs, are not allowed in the stadium, and all, including bags and backpacks are left at identifiable places in a pile by the entrance of the stadium.

Security measures at the Trump rallies can also be quite intimidating. A seasoned traveller will know about the airport security drills – that's is the level of security to expect. None of the supporters mind at all – it is much needed for Trump's security – these are die hard supporters that would take the proverbial bullet for their Trump.

Once inside the arena, food and drinks can be bought and eaten, and as people look around the already packed arena for available seats, the harmony continues with shouts of, "There's two over here!" or "Here's a spare one!"

Music and various speakers would warm up the crowd as they await the arrival of Trump. And when it is time to welcome President Trump – euphoria would fill the whole arena as mobile phones flare up to hopefully capture well focused images in between the obstructions of red caps.

Trump simply enjoys himself, he is in his element, and he has the energy of a 35-year old and would stand and speak for over one hour.

After over one hour, it will all be over, the president would have left the building and the followers would depart for home, with sore throats from screaming, 'build the wall', 'four more years', 'we love Trump', 'Drain the Swamp', at the various appropriate intervals to show for the entertainment.

On their way out of the auditorium, and still high from the exciting entertainment; bags and backpacks etc. are retrieved, with contents intact, from the identifiable spot that they were left.

The number of people that attempted to reserve seats for President Trump's first rally since the coronavirus outbreak was unusually high with more than 1 million people requesting tickets for the Tulsa, Oklahoma, event that was held on Saturday, June 21st, 2020. Attendees had their temperatures checked upon arrival to mitigate the possible spread of the coronavirus and rally goers were also provided with masks and hand sanitizer. The organisers had planned an outdoor rally for an anticipated overflow crowd that did not materialize – the Democrats had used hundreds of teenage TikTok users and K-pop fans to book the tickets. The fire marshal counted 6,200 scanned tickets of attendees instead of the 19,000 capacity.

Trump, the ultimate showman is hilarious, outrageous, bold and flamboyant – they crowd love it. He utterly ruthlessly takes down his critics and the latest fake news reported – as he slashes and dispels every bit of their reports and he does this with Byronic tongue-lashing style – it is an experience.

Trump would now have to put defensive hijacking measures in place for future rallies. As the election month looms, I am not certain that there will be future Trump rallies because of knowing the social distancing rules as prescribed by the democrats, although BLM and Antifa can crowd out the streets protesting and rioting

11

TAKING ON THE INVISIBLE ENEMY

No one believes that the coronavirus that has been around for over 40 years. The hoax is treating a virus with a 99.5% survival rate as if fatality was worse than Ebola or even 2009 H1N1 when the democrats and Obama were in office.

Before the COVID-19 lockdown, the Democrats and the mainstream media had ran out of campaign talking points such as no school shootings, no migrant caravans at the southern border, fighting in Syria winding down, North Korea not firing missiles and Trump vanquishing the sham impeachment, with their mantra 'never let a serious crisis go to waste', the coronavirus gave them a new scam to attack the president.

The world has had several recent deadly pandemics, the last one was the 2009 H1H1, and it is obvious that even Pelosi did not expect the pandemic to involve a lockdown. Fuelled by the mainstream media, they decided to lockdown the economy in order to cause maximum damage and to crush the people in order to remove the president.

The president had stated during a January rally that,

"...they'll try anything, they'll try it over and over. They'd been doing it since we got in. It's all turning. They lost. It's all turning. Think of it. Think of it. And this is their new hoax."

The coronavirus scheme played out as usual as if taken from a strategy document;

- control the population with fear-mongering and panic,
- use the mainstream media,
- Spread propaganda.

In February 2020, the president announced that 2.5 million of mostly African Americans and Latin American ethnic minorities were in full time employment, unemployment rate held steady decreased to a low 3.9% and average wages were nearly 3% higher than they were a year ago. Following the announcement, Obama then tweeted on February 19th; "When you hear how great the economy is doing right now, let's just remember when this recovery started."

And then came COVID-19 which brought the economy to zero level, lock down measures, as stay-at-home orders and social distancing orders. 2.5 million People were registered as unemployed as employers laid off staff, and lifting the 'lockdown' to open up the economy would mean that Trump will be starting from a very clean slate.

The Trump administration's response is far different from the picture that the media and the Democrats tried to paint. When the World Health Organization was first alerted to the virus, the Democrats were in the middle of their impeachment witch hunt, but Trump was taking action immediately to protect the Americans.

With absolute foresight after the impeachment in February during his rally, Trump had stated that,

"We have exposed the far left's corruption and defeated their sinister schemes and let's see what happens in the coming months," he carried on, "let's watch. Let's just watch. Very dishonest people."

THE WEEKS BEFORE COVID-19 LOCKDOWN

The COVID-19 economic crash may well pan out on the president's advantage, because the Democrats had attributed the pre-coronavirus economic boom to Obama. Right up to February, he had no opposition, but he ran against the impact of COVID-19, its collateral damage and its ripple effects, with all three disasters running simultaneously.

The COVID-19 pandemic was a totally new virus that caught every one out. It came from China and in order to save face the early months were riddled with a series of cover up mechanisms, as they hoped to understand it, contain it and put controls in place and then use an appropriate time to inform the world. As such, China lied, the WHO hid it and the world's experts continued to give varying advice. Until the president began his occasional comments and remarks which the main stream media and the Democrats either deliberately chose to ignore in order to escalate the crisis in line with their signature policy 'never let a serious crisis go to waste' or were completely not able to grasp the most basic indications that for three months something was amiss in China, Thailand and several other countries.

The Democrats had continued to use the experts to play down the crisis however, the president was astute enough to realise that they were giving conflicting advice because the virus was totally unknown – perhaps the reason why they did not fire either Fauchi or Deborah Birx

Six months from the outbreak, we are being told that coronavirus is here to stay and will change our lifestyles, even after a vaccination has been developed, tested and approved for use.

When President Trump imposed the China Travel Public Health Entry Screening to US airports on January 17th, he was branded 'racists and xenophobic', by the mainstream media and the Democrats.

Speaker Pelosi continued to reemphasis that the threats of the pandemic were all about the president trying to deflect and distract the world from the looming impeachment by creating fear of some virus, which the WHO had attested could only be transmitted by eating dogs, cats and pangolins in China. Here was Pelosi directly putting the lives of American's at risk and in fact to a greater extent, the world.

PLAYING DOWN THE PANDEMIC DURING (SOTU)

The Democrats continually played down the concerns about the pandemic.

At the beginning of each calendar year, the US president delivers an annual message to the members of the Congress in what they call the State of the Union

Address (SOTU), which is a report that includes a budget message and an economic report of the nation.

The 2020 State of the Union Address on February 4th 2020 began at 9:00 p.m. EST and was televised and streamed by all major US and UK broadcast television networks. The date for the address fell one day after the Iowa caucuses in the 2020 presidential election, and one day before the Senate vote on whether or not to convict Trump in his impeachment trial and as the address concluded, Pelosi tore up her copy of the speech in four separate sections. The rather vulgar and discourteous act was played out to the world, and for all to see the most contemptible act applauded one side of the hall seated by mainly the Democrats.

As the world rushed to condemn the Speaker, social media went into the most furious frenzy and she was derided with every adjective imaginable.

Pelosi defends her actions, by stating that as soon as the president entered the room, he refused her handshake, and when the condemnations poured in, her reasons changed, she alluded to the contents of the speech being lies.

She had not only torn up Trump's State of the Union Address on February 4th in a fiendish hate which many confirmed was not only disrespectful to the various persons it was directed to, but it was also illegal because she had violated the Presidential Records Act or other statutes governing the Maintenance of Federal records. Also, the Speaker had torn up details of what the President had heralded 'the great American comeback', which primarily focused on national security, the economy, health care, and foreign policy. In just three years, jobs were booming, incomes soaring, poverty was plummeting, crime rate was falling and the country was thriving.

The torn-up speech had unfortunately included a strong concern about the pandemic. The president was already beginning to put strategies in place and had commented that,

---

"Working closely together on the Coronavirus outbreak in China. My administration will take all necessary steps to safeguard our citizens from this threat."

In another occasion, having championed religious liberty, the president called for greater religious freedoms, such as strengthening prayer in public schools and also declared a National Day of Prayer on March 15th in the face of the pandemic, for all those affected by the coronavirus outbreak, of which House of Rep. Rashida Tlaib unleashed a profanity-laced attack when she immediately retweeted a post on Twitter which said in part "F**k a National day of prayer".

Rashida Tlaib was applauded by the mainstream media, and other Democrats, playing down the severity of the virus.

CHINATOWN

Pelosi and the Democrats had not been done putting the American and UK people's lives at risk. Despite the president's flight restriction on January 17th and total travel ban on the January 30th, Pelosi continually denigrated Trump's COVID-19 concerns when she toured San Francisco's Chinatown on February 27th 2020 to send the message,

> "...there's no reason tourists or locals should be staying away from the area because of coronavirus concerns. that's what we're trying to do today is to say everything is fine here, come because precautions have been taken. The city is on top of the situation."

Both UK and US mainstream media– including our BBC and LBC in the United Kingdom were forceful in supporting the mass public gatherings.

This confirmed that Nancy Pelosi did not consider the global pandemic to involve a lockdown or simply intended to endanger the lives of the people.

The Trump hate was so imbued enough to make Nancy Pelosi, to make the publicized stop in Chinatown to implore people to 'please come and visit and enjoy Chinatown'. She continued imploring all residents to 'Come to Chinatown' and further went on to convincing all that 'it is OK to be in Chinatown.' "We know that there is concern surrounding tourism, traveling all throughout the world, but we think it's very safe to be in Chinatown and hope that others will come, she had continued. "It's lovely here."

That global media publicity was to prove catastrophic in the numbers of infections that was soon to ravage the state of California.

PLAYING DOWN THE PANDEMIC MARDI GRAS NEW ORLEANS

Another high-profile event that the Democrats used to kill off their citizens was the New Orleans Mardi Gras celebrations which attracted over 1.4 million revellers. This event played a direct role in spreading the virus from Louisiana to the other parts of the Nation as revellers travelled back to their destinations.

Around February 27th, still being convinced by the experts, the Governors of Louisiana and Mayor of New Orleans ignored the president's travel restrictions and eventual travel bans of the January 30th and relaxed their guard.

They would not cancel the '2020 New Orleans Mardis Gras' carnival which was also to prove catastrophic. About 1.4 million people had travelled from afar and had to travel back to their various towns, a very high number of infected people carried with them the corona virus which subsequently infected the people at their home towns.

Governor John Bel Edwards believed that Mardi Gras had a lot to do with the number of coronavirus cases in the New Orleans metro area.

BRISTOL YOUTH 4

Not wanting to be left out in playing down the president's concerns, the UK mainstream media joined as they egged on and supported the Soros sponsored 16-year-old Greta Thunberg when she gathered over 30,000 children in the Bristol Youth Strike 4 Climate (BYS4C) event, on February 28th.

Greta had originally intended to visit London, but Trafalgar Square was considered too small for the rally, so the event was moved to Bristol.

The police stated that around 15,000 had attended, but the media reported that attendance was about 30,000.

The climate campaign had cost Bristol council more than £10,000 and the irony of the 'green' related rally which was not covered by the mainstream media was that the generation supposed to save the climate had caused an enormous amount of destruction in Bristol. The grass on the site was damaged and it cost a further £25,000 to repair. Also, a prudent number of infections from the 30,000 that attended would be over 500,000, based on projections according to Dr Robin Thompson, a junior research fellow in mathematical epidemiology and mathematical modelling expert from Oxford University;

- Without social distancing, one coronavirus sufferer could, in six weeks, have started chains of transmission with 1,093 cases.
- With social distancing, the chains of transmission would involve 127 cases.

CDC EXPERTS PLAYED IT DOWN

Despite the Democrats and mainstream media playing it down, even the virologists and experts weren't ready for the new pandemic, until it hit them with the president's travel restrictions comments around January 17th. The president went for the worse-case scenario option of there being a 'full pandemic' and got the experts to work around that.

The outbreak of pneumonia came just a few weeks before China's busiest travel season of the year and people travelling into China were warned to avoid animals and contact with sick people as the country grappled with the mystery 'pneumonia' outbreak, this was before China's busiest travel season of the year, when millions of people take buses, trains and planes for the Lunar New Year.

The upcoming holiday had prompted concerns in Taiwan, where the Premier Chen Chimaivice had urged the island's health and welfare ministry to strengthen quarantine controls at airports and 'plan properly', and advised their residents planning to travel to or near Wuhan to wear masks and avoid contact with wild animals.

The viral outbreak was reported to be in Wuhan, the central Chinese city with a population of over 11 million, which by now had at least 59 cases.

Chinese health officials had ruled out a resurgence of the highly contagious SARS virus, which had killed thousands more than a decade ago, after fears spread online that it had made a comeback.

No one at this stage was given the true nature or extent of the virus, however, a 'be aware and practice usual precautions,' health alert was issued, which also urged US citizens to seek medical care 'right away' if they felt sick after travelling to Wuhan.

Independent reports from the surrounding countries' CDC experts confirmed at the time that although the 'outbreak was under control', it was best to take care. It was also reported that 'so far, none of the 59 patients infected with pneumonia had died though seven are seriously ill', but all were being treated in quarantine and no obvious evidence of human-to-human transmission had been found so far.

China then stopped all the planes coming into China, but the very wicked thing they did was to leave their people to travel abroad which infected the world. They could have stopped the spread or perhaps had deliberately let it spread and to make things worse, the WHO turned a blind eye.

CONFUSED EXPERTS GOT IT ALL WRONG

A World Health Organization official had even suspected human-to-human transmission of the novel coronavirus as early as Mid-December 2019. Also, viral respiratory disease specialist Doctor Maria Van Kerkhove confirmed that since there was a cluster of pneumonia, and that the virus was a respiratory pathogen, this meant that there had to be human-to-human transmission but both the WHO and the Chinese authorities strenuously denied any suggestion of human-to-human transmission for weeks until mid-January 2020, after president Trump correctly decided to impose travel restriction of the country.

Despite Van Kerkhove's apparent suspicions, the WHO Chief Tedros, downplayed the possibility that the virus could spread between people, and infact, assured the world repeatedly that Wuhan healthcare workers weren't becoming infected with coronavirus.

Another doctor, Lu Xiaohong mentioned in a press report that by Christmas she had already heard of doctors becoming infected with the virus. Another doctor, Li Wenliang was punished for warning the public about the virus, and the WHO continued asserting that there was no evidence that the virus could be transmitted from humans. Their January 13th press release further stated that,

"...to date, there has been no suggestion of human to human transmission of this new coronavirus" and "...there have been no infections reported among health care workers, which can be an early indicator of person to person spread."

They even tweeted on January 14th that,

"...preliminary investigations conducted by the Chinese authorities have found no clear evidence of human-to-human transmission of the novel corona-virus identified in Wuhan, China" and "...to date, China has not reported any cases of infection among healthcare workers or contacts of the cases. Based on the available information there is no clear evidence of human-to-human transmission."

Doctor Maria Van Kerkhove soon changed her suspicions and on January 14th, acknowledged that,

"...it is possible that there is limited human-to-human transmission, potentially among families, it is very clear right now that we have no sustained human-to-human transmission."

TEDROS PLAYED IT DOWN

Tedros Adhanom Ghebreyesus, the public health researcher and official has been engulfed in corruption and incompetence ever before he became Director-General of the World Health Organization.

Back in May 2017, Tedros, then the leading candidate to head the World Health Organization was accused of covering up three cholera epidemics in his home country, Ethiopia, when he was health minister — a charge that should have seriously undermined his campaign to run the agency.

Dr Tedros at the time was a senior officer of the organized crime syndicate for the Tigray People's Liberation Front (TPLF), the gangster mafia that ruled Ethiopia from 1991-2018.

Within that role, he also served as Health Minister and Foreign Minister, for the brutal regime in Somali, the most corrupt genocidal regimes.

Tedros was complicit in the TPLF's crime of genocide against the Somali people of the Ogaden, with the genocidal blockade of food and medicine to the region, and was also responsible for expelling the Red Cross and Doctors from Ogaden.

Now in 2020, he found himself on the hot seat with the corona virus pandemic raging which confirmed that he was totally incapable and incompetent for the role.

HOW TEDROS AND CHINA HID THE PANDEMIC

To get a better grasp on how China carried out their deception, egged on by the Democrats and the mainstream media, with their undertaking 'never to let a serious crisis go to waste', we have to go back to the closing months of 2019 when they never uttered any concerns about the outbreak, which they accused the president of creating in order to deflect their impeachment scam.

Around January 1st 2020, almost thirty days before China's admission that a new virus had been identified, credible reports confirmed that nearly 200 people were infected and the first cracks in China's story were already beginning to form.

By January 1st, all the laboratories involved with the novel coronavirus were ordered to destroy their samples, eliminating vital information and hurling researchers back to square one. The World Health Organization soon stepped up to cover for China, parroting that the virus was not contagious and that there was nothing to worry about.

With the apparent all-clear signal sounded loud and clear to the world by the WHO, on January 18th, (Note that the president's travel restrictions were on the January 17th), Wuhan went along a record-breaking open banquet, where around 40,000 families cooked and prepared dishes to celebrate the event's 20th anniversary. Millions of people were expected to attend the new world record event for being the largest food festival.

Life in China largely continued as it normally and more than 5 million people were allowed to leave the city just a week before then and days later, however, the government could no longer hide the severity of the outbreak. On the

January 22nd, less than a week after the banquet, the world was horrified to hear that six Chinese cities had been placed under a full lockdown.

As if the lies were not enough, Beijing had "vacuumed up" masks and personal protective equipment before the communist country let the world know how dangerous the coronavirus was.

Meanwhile, ignoring their reporting obligations, China pressured the WHO into misleading the world when the virus was first discovered.

The Tedros even met with Chinese President Xi Jinping on January 28th, 2020 which served to provide the mainstream media with their racist and xenophobic taunts at president Trump. The publicity photos clearly deceived the whole world – except of course Donald Trump who with his usual defiant stance, continued with a full China ban on the January 30th.

The World Health Organization shockingly fought against the travel restrictions, placing China's own economy above the health of the world. Videos of Chinese people collapsing on the street soon went viral with reports of hospitals soon being overloaded, the number of dead soared and soon, swarms of crows hinted that even the mortuaries were bursting.

WHO officials weren't content to just defend China's economic interests, but actually began praising the country to deflect any criticism especially from Trump,

"We are encouraged that the steps China has taken to contain the outbreak at its source appear to have bought the world time, even though those steps have come at greater cost to China itself."

Dr Deborah Birx, the response coordinator for the White House Coronavirus Task Force, further suggested that the US response to the pandemic may not have been as effective as possible due to "missing" data from China, she continued,

---

"The medical community interpreted the Chinese data as serious, but smaller than anyone expected ....because, probably...we were missing a significant amount of the data, now that we see what happened to Italy and we see what happened to Spain." Doctor Deborah Birx went on national television to explain how China's lack of transparency allowed the coronavirus to "fan... across the globe."

In effect, China could have prevented 95% of coronavirus infections if it had acted sooner to stem the outbreak.

By the time the WHO acknowledged evidence of human-to-human transmission, on January 22nd, the president had already ordered travel restrictions, ordered screening and quarantines at five major airports. Around this date the US had already detected its first coronavirus case.

Beijing did not act responsibly – and in retaliation to the president's early response, Beijing had 'vacuumed up' masks and personal protective equipment before they would let the world know the extent of the danger from the virus.

As the days sped on, the world requested antibodies' tests kit, to be used to test for the presence of antibodies to know if a person had developed an immune response to the virus. These test kits sent by China were of very poor quality and provided false readings. White House adviser Peter Navarro had stated that,

> When it came to containing the spread of the coronavirus, they hid it for six weeks, they could have contained it in Wuhan."

Another expert Dr Li Meng-Yan, a specialist in virology at Hong Kong's School of Public Health who fled to the US says that she "clearly assessed" that Coronavirus was created or possibly modified in a lab linked to the People's Liberation Army. However, Beijing has denied the allegations. Dr Li-Meng said

> , "At that time, I had clearly assessed that the virus came from a Chinese Communist Party military lab. The Wuhan wet market was just used as a decoy."

She stressed that when she reported her findings to her superiors, she was not taken seriously and ignored. Before speaking out, she fled to the US in April 2020, from Hong Kong fearing for her safety and claimed that she had to leave because of 'how the Chinese authorities treated whistle-blowers in order to conceal an epidemic'

12

EARLY DECISIVE ACTIONS

Here, I have summarised the key leadership and decisive actions taken by President Trump from the onset of the coronavirus pandemic and how the Democrats and the mainstream media persisted in their almost reflex reaction to be critical of just about every action that he took, instead of cooperating to reduce the impact of the flu-like virus that was rumoured to be coming from the wet market at Wuhan China.

Many Chinese people were meant to travel to and from China for their New Year celebrations which ran from January 21st to February 20th and around January 8th,

---

"Thai doctors diagnosed another Chinese traveller with mild pneumonia on January 8th, later confirmed to have been caused by the new virus."

On January 19th, it was reported that a 35-year-old man admitted himself to Snohomish County, Washington, with a 4-day history of cough and fever. On checking into the clinic, the patient put on a mask in the waiting room. He stated that he had returned to Washington State on January 15th after traveling to visit family in Wuhan, China.

The patient said that he had seen a health alert from the US Centers for Disease Control and Prevention (CDC) about the novel coronavirus outbreak in China and, because of his symptoms and recent travel, decided to see a health care provider, but relied on the WHO experts that requested specimen collection, and the patient was discharged to home isolation with active monitoring by the local health department.

RACIST XENOPHOBE FOR ORDERING FLIGHT RESTRICTION

Convinced that many of the Chinese travellers coming back from the Chinese New Year celebrations were likely to have partaken in the delicacies, and in the furore and commotion of the impeachment hoax, President Trump decided to impose 'flight restrictions' from China, with checks on any foreign national who had travelled to and from China in the last fourteen days as a result of the China New Year celebrations. This decisive action was to prevent the spread of the novel coronavirus, which had already infected 10,000 people in twenty-four countries, and had killed 213 people in China.

The aim here was also to restrict and direct all flights into seven airports to facilitate and consolidate passenger screening and evaluation.

The President was soon accused of being a racist xenophobe by the democrats and mainstream media, who as we know have a reflex action for aggressively attacking every action he makes. Trump stood his ground, the global leadership move which other countries were soon to follow. He was already being attacked for his stance against the Chinese tech giant Huawei, then having to call the virus the 'Chinese flu', and now the travel restriction order on China.

RACIST XENOPHOBE FOR ORDERING COMPLETE TRAVEL BAN

Being Trump, he would not stop there, it seemed to the left and their mainstream media that they had really got him this time for having such a dislike and prejudice against the Chinese people, on the January 30th, he went for a complete travel ban.

Despite the President's flight restrictions, New York, a global travel hub did not heed the ban. The Democrats, with the full backing of the media loved the Governor or of New York's stance against President Trump. The attack served great for them to alter the course of the elections. However, the decision not to heed the President was to prove catastrophic in the number of infections that was soon to ravage the state of New York and the surrounding environs.

As the virus continued to ravage the world, Trump being Trump, did not seem bothered about the Democrat and media frenzy and support for China – Trump still would not back down on the travel restrictions and went for the full measure complete ban.

Trump did not stop there, he further announcement that US taxpayer funding to the World Health Organization would be temporarily withheld, pending a thorough investigation, because of the organization's assistance to the Chinese communist regime in covering up and downplaying the extent of the coronavirus crisis in the crucial early stages of the outbreak.

The mainstream media and the democrats were now beside themselves. Rancorous by bitterness and resentment, they claimed that the President was deflecting from the impeachment.

They were aghast at withholding the WHO funding, the bulk of which went to line the pocket of the Somalia chairman, Tedros Adhanom Ghebreyesus, that I was later to discover that China was instrumental to his appointment.

In lashing out at Trump over the travel bans and suspension of WHO funding, however, Pelosi and the Democrats all left themselves wide open for entirely justifiable criticism for their actions or rather, inactions due to their partisan "games and gimmicks" which left the United States the epicenter of the novel COVID-19 and the thousands of deaths that was to follow.

CHINA–CENTRIC; WHY WOULD WE CALL IT A PANDEMIC?

Six months on, the Democrats have not commented on how the WHO had acted against the USA but rather encouraged Tedros and gave him media coverage. WHO are not supposed to take sides or favour nations, however, the pandemic exposed the organization and their staff to be absolutely China-centric, which began two years before the pandemic when Tedros Ghebreyesus met with the most senior of Chinese officials.

Tedros had been impressed by the state of China's Belt and Road but was especially fond of the country's medical industry, which promised to dump medical aid into African countries, the flood of which seemed to take a major responsibility off the WHO's back, although they were funded to do so, but they no longer had to provide the aid medication.

The World Health Organization went along with China's claims and also denied human-to-human transmission of the virus despite concern from South Korea and Thailand.

Also, the Chinese had advised the WHO director to announce that,

"Unless we're convinced it's uncontrollable, why (would) we call it a pandemic?"

A detailed timeline showed that China had 'evidence of human-human transmission from early December', but continued to deny it could spread this way until January 20th – three days after President Trump ignored mainstream media abuses of being 'a racist and xenophobic' and insisted on screening Chinese travellers at the five airports.

In retaliation, here is what China did, they imposed travel bans on people traveling throughout the nation, but continued to tell the rest of the world that travel bans were unnecessary.

By the end of March 2020, it soon emerged that the actions taken by China were causing concerns, which made the President to criticize the WHO as, "slow to respond to the crises', and repeatedly said the organization had been 'China-centric."

The President complained that, "It was wrong that the WHO receives vast amounts of money from the United States', and indicated that he 'will consider putting a hold on funding The World Health Organization's funding because, we must stop funding organizations that hate us.'

PUNISHMENT FOR IMPOSING TRAVEL RESTRICTIONS

Testing in the United States became prolifically abundant, and, statistically, if President Trump had not imposed the screening as early as January 17th, the number of COVID-19 deaths to the number of people tested and infected would have exceeded the ratios predicted by the experts to be above 3.4%. As of June 30th, it was 0.049%. China had also 'vacuumed up' masks and personal protective equipment before allowing the WHO to let the world know how dangerous the coronavirus was in China.

We all know that the WHO had insisted on the US working with China, because China 'understood' the virus and had been working on the virus for a while. Antibody tests were greatly needed and being the source of the out-break, the world expected to get the tests from China, but what they sent were very low quality unusable anti bodies –the test readings were either false or did not make sense.

China decided to punish the US further by sending counterfeit test kits, which crucially disrupted the US's efforts to stem the virus. The implications of this could have been worse, if Trump had not decided to ignore the WHO's advice and set about commissioning various firms to manufacture US made test kits, which greatly served Trump's campaign promise of bringing all manufacturing back to the US.

What is important is not how the disease started but rather what Beijing did in response to it. The timeline showed that the outbreak was hidden from the world with the help of the WHO for six weeks, and although China had deliberately destroyed evidence about the start and source, leaked documents reportedly confirmed evidence of human-to-human transmission as far back as November 2019, Beijing did nothing until January 20th 2020 following Trump kicking up a 'global fuss'.

Most crucial of all, the virus could have been contained in Wuhan and the regions surrounding the area, however, they allowed travelling out of the area which infected the world, but banned people coming into China.

Many commentators have given their views on the pandemic, but agree on the same premise that China:

- "Maliciously spread the virus with an 'unthinkable' secret plot to 'even the playing field' on the world stage."
- "Tried to deceive the world into thinking that it was not human to human transmission."
- "The US Democrats and CNN made things even worse by berating and

playing out their 'usual' hatred following the President's January 17th 'screen and possibly quarantine' order."

- "Even Joe Biden finally agreed that re-establishing supply chains for critical health care equipment and supplies in America 'is an absolute national security priority."

When you put these facts together, you come to an unthinkable conclusion.

Several publications soon emerged, such as the 'Intelligence Community' which concluded that China concealed the extent of the Wuhan coronavirus outbreak in the country. The report further stated that China intentionally lowered its reported number of coronavirus cases.

On May 18th 2020, it was reported that China admitted that it ordered labs to destroy virus samples, which set the world at least eight weeks back and caused loss of lives. They cited safety and bureaucracy as its reasons, Liu Dengfeng of the Chinese National Health Commission's science and education department confirmed that China's government ordered the destruction of samples of the coronavirus was in order to cover up the extent of how dangerous the pandemic was in order to, "...prevent the risk to laboratory biological safety and prevent secondary disasters caused by unidentified pathogens."

THE WHO IS NO LONGER FIT FOR PURPOSE

Despite Democrats and media objections, several countries that had had one or two tiffs with China and knew that they were not to be trusted began imposing full or limited travel bans on China, these included the Philippines, the Bahamas, Mongolia, and Singapore. The above prompted my re-tweet of the President's message that, "...the WHO is No Longer Fit for Purpose."

That message sent the mainstream media in an enraged frenzy. Being Trump, he did not just stop at the assault on the WHO's integrity. The President that he would cease the funding of the World Health Organisation for not only being China-Centric but also because it was financially pragmatic to doing so for three main reasons;

- The USA funded the WHO by an annual $420 million in 2019. By the end of May 2020, Death 70,000. Population 328 million.
- China funded the WHO annually with only $40 million, they had provided a coronavirus death figure of only 4,890 Population of 1.3 billion.
- The WHO had aided China with all their lies, cover ups and dis-information and had caused deaths all over the world, with highest death numbers in the USA – their largest contributors.

The President would not stop there;

"We have deep concerns over whether America's generosity has been put to the best use possible."

"...the WHO failed to adequately keep the international community aware of the threat of the coronavirus."

"The WHO failed in this duty, and must be held accountable."

"The WHO had ignored "credible information" in December 2019 that the virus could be transmitted from human to human."

Trump followed it with an announcement that he was suspending funding for the WHO — pending an investigation into its handling of the coronavirus pandemic.

The President's move prompted widespread criticism from the Democrats on Capitol Hill and international bodies including the European Union – not us in the UK – we left the EU just on time to be blinded, as House Speaker Nancy Pelosi blasted Trump's decision to freeze funding for the World Health Organization, vowing to "swiftly" challenge the action.

Realising that they had once again played into President's Trump's decisive actions, that avenue of attack suddenly stopped. Meanwhile, the villainous WHO Director-Tedros, who faced global calls to resign from his post amid the controversy, had the effrontery to issue a statement to counter the great President move with, "We regret the decision by the President of the US to order a hold on funding to WHO...we will work with our partners to fill any financial gaps we face and make sure work continues uninterrupted."

The UK is the next largest funders to the WHO, following the USA – at the time of writing, none of the other partners have yet to fill any financial gaps left by the USA.

NAMING THE VIRUS

In order to avoid stigmatisation of the country, on the February 11th 2020, the WHO announced "COVID-19" as the name of the new disease and had advised against terms that link the virus to China also, although evident that China knew that they had messed up they attempted a disinformation campaign who were suggesting that the American military was the source of the outbreak. The President was not having that.

However, at a news briefing, on March 17th, 2020 a reporter asked about a White House official using the term "Kung flu" which the President had no knowledge of, and she asked whether the President calling it a "Chinese virus" in a tweet endangering Asian-Americans.

The brash reporter at this time was feeling good that she had asked a 'gotcha' moment of a relevant question. The President dismissed her accusations that his use of the term 'Chinese virus' to refer to the coronavirus was racist.

In the House of Commons here in the UK, the then shadow foreign secretary Emily Thornberry felt that joining in would give her a moment of relevant and even said of Trump,

"Now he's calling it the foreign virus, blaming it on Europe for its spread and today blaming the origins of the virus on China."

Other hateful comments followed,

"President Trump attempted to shift blame for the spread of coronavirus to China by using the phrase 'Chinese virus."

Within hours, the media admonished the President with calls of being racist and xenophobic, undaunted Trump defiantly retorted that,

"I called it the Chinese flu because it comes from China," and in true Trump form, he continued, "It's not racist at all. It comes from China; that's why I want to be accurate."

The Hodge twins, avid die-hard Trump supporters even had Shirts for sale with "We call It the Chinese Virus. Because It Comes From China." He dismissed concerns that his language would lead to any harm.

In his defence, which Trump rarely needs, social media reaction from the Trump support base went to melt down, that the terms "Chinese virus" or "Wuhan virus" in reference to COVID-19 – was accurate, but it was not the accuracy that the haters were referring to, they were using the comment to apply their 'racist and xenophobic' slur on the President.

Trump's response would soon create a ricochet shield on the hateful mainstream media and set them up for self-abasement and degradation.

Little did the democrats and mainstream media realise that many senior democrats and mainstream media reporters had also referred to COVID-19 as 'Chinese flu', weeks before Trump mentioned it in a tweet on March 16th. Weeks after it was first discovered and started spreading, it had already amassed an impressive array of sobriquets, such as

- "Wuhan flu",
- "Wuhan coronavirus",
- "Chinese coronavirus",
- "2019-nCoV", and the rather long-winded
- "Wuhan seafood market pneumonia viruses".

Some clever person then responded with a montage of dozens of times the liberal media had used the same 'Chinese flu' label themselves, which included CNN's Jim Acousta, MSNBC reporters and even Joe Biden. As soon as this video went viral, that angle of attack suddenly stopped.

13

NEVER LET A SERIOUS CRISIS GO TO WASTE

I s the American cities were being infected with the virus and the Trump administration was fighting hard to counter the impact of the spread, the Democrats decided to put their mantra into practice. The Obama administration had left the cupboards bare of PPE and America, along with the rest of the world, has never been ready for a major disease outbreak.

MASKS HOAX

The Obama-Biden administration left the Strategic National Stockpile in dangerously short supply of N-95 respirator masks after deploying nearly all of them to combat the 2009 swine flu pandemic. There's no evidence that any effort was made to replenish the stockpile despite experts calling on the Obama-Biden Administration to do so.

At the start of the lockdown, there was a need for (PPE) Personal Protection Equipment, China was withholding supplies and when health officials announced that many of the masks that they decided to release were being rejected because they did not meet the required quality standards, the Democrats 'never let a serious crisis go to waste' were convinced that they had Trump this time and there was no end to the media attack. What they had not realised was that from as early as January 17th, the President was already sourcing and trying to get around manufacturing masks in the US. The company 3 million had their factory in China and were exporting masks abroad underhandedly to higher paying countries. The masks themselves are difficult to make because they require specialized equipment to meet stringent regulatory standards for the virus. The President had always wanted US manufacturing back in the US however and the excessive media barrage was his chance.

So, when the various laboratories revealed that the masks from China were not specialised for the virus, the required specification was already in place in the USA, and all that was needed was to redirect surgical masks manufactured abroad back to America for use in the battle against the coronavirus.

In a rude response, 3 million emphasized that it had gained approval to import 10 million masks from its facilities in 'China'. 3 million were insufferable and told the White House's that having to end its exports of N95 respirators, was not politically correct we all know what Trumps thinks of political correctness. They continued, that if other countries retaliated against the US for not sharing respirator supplies, 3 million argued, the US could soon end up with fewer masks than it had before.

The President later said in a tweet that 3M 'will have a big price to pay' for exporting masks much needed in the US.

Not sure how they felt that they could put a challenge to President Trump, or the 'reminder of the bodies in the swamp' but on April 2nd, the President invoked the Defence Production Act (DPA) to compel 3 million, one of the only companies that manufactured N95 masks in the US, to scale up production for the correct specification in the USA and by the end of the week, 3 million and two other companies Honeywell and Prestige Ameritech provided end-to-end production of medical-grade N95 masks in the US, and both were ramping up production.

It did not end there, in an effort to combat the shortage, the US Food and Drug Administration announced an ingenious idea of sterilizing the N95 masks in order to relieve the critical mask shortages by turning the single-use respirators into reusable products with the potential to sterilize 4 million masks per day nationwide. The WHO, which is part of the United Nations, remained in a confused state, with its credibility diminished, and under increased scrutiny. In a move to disprove global opinion, the WHO had posted and deleted a tweet in late April claiming that, "There's no evidence" that people with coronavirus antibodies who have already recovered are immune from the virus.'

THE VENTILATORS HOAX

In March, one of the most disturbing concerns of the pandemic was the reported shortage of ventilators. One well-publicized estimate, repeated by the Democrats and the media was that the US would need roughly one million ventilators.

Ventilators are expensive, complex machines that cannot be churned out in the thousands overnight like the masks. Ventilators, formerly known as respirators, are designed to help move breathable air in and out of the lungs in the event that a person is unable to breathe by themselves or their lungs are not operating at full capacity.

The Democrats again picked on 'never to let a serious crisis go to waste', supported Andy Slavitt, the former acting administrator of the Centers for Medicare and Medicaid Services, in pushing the panic attack button by announcing that hospitals were 'Out of Ventilators' – that was a fabrication.

Prior to this, on March 14th, he had tweeted, "...last night I was with state and local officials around the US, well into the night. By March 23rd many of our largest cities and hospitals are on course to be overrun with cases."

Here, he was pushing the leak to the media who would soon start their frantic attacks for ventilators and beds.

Almost overnight, irresponsible headlines sent shivers globally with headlines such as,

- "The ventilation shortage is here. Medication is next."
- "The prospect of doctors forced to choose who will live and die."
- "Many areas of the U.S. face hospital bed shortages."
- "As the number of coronavirus patients continues to mount, medical facilities across the country have run out of health-care workers, ventilators and even hospital beds."

New York Governor Andrew Cuomo became the loud speaker, he sounded the alarm for ventilators repeatedly and he acknowledged,

"I don't have a crystal ball but I desperately need 30,000 ventilators, maybe 40,000, but only have 12,000."

Trump, with foresight and grasp on the situation was to ask, "Why are those numbers of ventilators required?"

Meanwhile, instead of communicating and appealing in private to the President, the New York Governor Andrew Cuomo appeared in a press filled room to report that the state had 'only six days' worth of ventilators left in its stockpile.

He used the press conference to report frantically with watery eyes at Trump for ventilators. Trumps immediately sent 400 with assurances that 4000 more ventilators would be delivered in the next four weeks.

Democrat governor Cuomo had protested that, "that was not good enough... We need 30,000 ventilators now!"

That was a direct vilification on the integrity of the President. However damaging that sounded and looked, Trump had a hunch that the lack of ventilators had to be associated with something dubious, so he set out not only to expose their scam, but also to embarrass them in the full glare of the global mainstream media.

From absolutely nowhere, the great President put his plan into action and added to a tweet, "...why those numbers of ventilators were required."

Call it common sense or sheer genius, he believed that government officials in New York are overestimating how many ventilators the state will need to treat patients diagnosed with the coronavirus. He tweeted, "I don't believe you need 40,000 or 30,000 ventilators. You go into major hospitals sometimes; they'll have two ventilators. And now all of a sudden, they're saying, "Can we order 30,000 ventilators?" really?"

Cuomo and the mainstream media, including the BBC immediately berated the President for not being able to supply ventilators and was, "sick to suggest that "some ventilators were found", and "he's done it this time."

The subject of ventilators turned political, when multiple establishment media outlets accused Trump of downplaying the need for the devices.

There were headlines like, "the President dismissed pleas for thousands of life-saving ventilators from Democratic governors in states hit hard by the new coronavirus."

"No big deal! Just the President of the United States suggesting that the Governor of New York is lying about the number of ventilators he needs to help keep people alive!"

It was obvious that Cuomo was using the issue of ventilators to try and harm President Trump politically. The media was relentless,

"What proof did Trump offer to back up this claim? Um, none,"

CNN's Chris Cillizza wrote.

But as Cuomo and other civic leaders joined the media in calling for more of the devices, Trump pointed out that, "New York already has thousands of them in storage."

The mainstream media erupted that the President was making unsubstantiated retaliatory punches.

The media fell for this trap, they went manic for several days on their wall to wall 'attack the President' news commentaries.

The President who thrives on attacks and assaults by now could neither contain nor help himself – he simply had to go for another thrashing with,

"...did thousands of Federal Government (delivered) Ventilators find in New York storage NY must distribute NOW...

As I put my hands on my head with, 'Dear God, they have eventually got something on the President – Holy mother help the President, they've got him this time."

That made the mainstream media delirious – the BBC and LBC felt they had 'had him this time'. Supporters group chats went eerily quiet with nerves with absolutely no posts as the mainstream media headlines condemned him for daring to accuse the governor and hospitals of stealing ventilators in order to cover up for his own incompetence of not having crucial ventilators in place.

The media were left to stew for several more days and then, it was revealed that several warehouses had stashed away ventilators. Watch this! What happened next was such a shock, New York Governor Andrew Cuomo admitted that his state already had thousands of unused ventilators even as he and the establishment media attacked President Donald Trump over the supposed shortage of the potentially life-saving medical devices.

Many experts even commented at this time that the hospitals in the state did not need all those numbers of ventilators – "not even from their projections of infections."

The media goading abruptly stopped almost one week later because almost simultaneously, the New York Governor Cuomo cowered in his briefing which was rather painful to watch when he admitted that his rabid attack on the President about there being serious shortage of ventilators was because he felt he would need more,

He had predicted the state would run out of ventilators in six days 'at the current burn rate.'

"...Yes, they're in a stockpile because that's where they're supposed to be because we don't need them yet. We need them for the apex."

Speaking at his daily news briefing on March 27th, the Democratic Governor then admitted that he had unused ventilators in a "stockpile."

"We have ventilators in a stockpile. We just don't need them yet. Hospitals say they desperately need them now!"

So, they did have a stockpile of ventilators, however, three days before, it was a different story, until the President had caught them all out.

But on April 6th, Cuomo, possibly after the President had offered to expose more burial sites of the bodies buried by Cuomo went on to admit, "We're OK, and we have some in reserve."

Just like that, after the embarrassing revelation, the bombardment from the media on ventilators suddenly ceased.

Cuomo had 1,750 ventilators stockpiled, and a total number of 8,991 ventilators were available in the state at the time.

President Trump was aware that Cuomo's state had thousands of unused ventilators not yet placed in hospitals.

Within hours, Cuomo was forced to admit that the President was right and then added – it seemed to me that the President had squeezed the full truth unreservedly from him conjuring up the thoughts that the President 'knows where the bodies are buried'.

"Yes, they're in a stockpile because that's where they're supposed to be because we don't need them yet. We need them for the apex." "We're ok, and we have some in reserve."

The President did not just sit back at that, no one realised that Trump had over reached the experts' projections for the need for ventilators and by the end of April, the President then applied his business strategic genius. Having identified the global shortages and demand and as part of his economic recovery deals, he decided not only to manufacture for home consumption but to trade to the world at large.

The United States were literally making trade deals, exporting ventilators to various countries.

Also, even before Cuomo's announcement, New Jersey reported that 46% of its ventilators were still available.

That angle of attack suddenly stopped being broadcast by the media as group chats began posting that hospitals remained underutilised and in fact, the Ships were never used – the experts' projections of the numbers of patients were way far off.

With all these 'Cuomo' goings on, there was another scare brewing in the UK – our Prime Minister was admitted on Sunday, April 5th to an NHS hospital in central London for tests ten days after confirming he had contracted coronavirus around March 28th. He still had persistent symptoms and was admitted at the advice of his doctor.

As the days rolled us on into the 'lockdown and social distancing' several events quite mirrored the decisions being taken in the US; like toilet paper and various cupboard food grocery hoarding, the advice given on the supply chain of stocks, the truckers that worked so hard to get the goods into the stores, etc.

From mid-March, both countries were encouraged to follow the 'lockdown' guidelines to slow the spread, which included;

- enhanced personal hygiene suggestions
- working from home
- social distancing
- cough etiquette
- minimizing face to face meetings
- sanitizing hands on entry into work and many other places

THE HOSPITAL BEDS HOAX

As for the bed shortages, Andy Slavitt, the former acting administrator of the Centers for Medicare and Medicaid Services, that had pushed the panic attack button by announcing that,

"...the number of coronavirus patients continues to mount, medical facilities across the country have run out of health-care workers, ventilators and even hospital beds."

In the President's style of letting people eat their own words, no one knew that he was years ahead in preparing for the beds, as always, he uses the haters to justify his policies instead of the protracted holdups in order 'never to let a serious crisis go to waste.

Even before the comment was made, Trump was already in meetings with the armed forces to make beds ready for dispatch to any hospital that needed them.

The President did not stop there. He went further and announced that on March 18th, he had already deployed two army navy hospital ships; USNS

Comfort and USNS Mercy. He also announced that both were in fact equipped and waiting to set sail to relieve in particular the epicenter of the virus, New York's overwhelmed hospitals if needed.

Trump boasted that the ship had been ready weeks before the Pentagon initially thought it could be, as he touted his response to the coronavirus outbreak.

Another scam that was discovered was that before the pandemic, many hospitals at the time were closing down because of lack of funds, but all of a sudden, respirators were being demanded and used unnecessarily for patients that had come in for mere anxiety.

These patients were given '...the choice of getting vented or taking the risk of being dead from the virus.'

The option was easily accepted and they were killed off and body bagged by the end of the day from being vented.

Having people vented made so much financial sense because, all New York hospitals received $13,000 for every COVID-19 diagnosis and $39,000 for every person put on a ventilator, all of which explained why ventilators were in such high demand in the USA during the early stages of the coronavirus hysteria.

It was even reported that a hospital that had been closed for over one year had fraudulently received $121,722, with no beds and no patients.

DEATH RATE HOAX

The President had described the pandemic as 'as an invisible' enemy which very much suited the Democrats who have used all the events associated with the virus to attack the Trump administration.

Around the end of March 2020, the US COVID-19 infections had surpassed the unqualified figures of China and the US was now leading the world in the highest number of deaths. The Democrats had never contributed in any way whatsoever to assist in this fight against the virus. They were so hyped up at the sight of the country being ravaged by the virus.

With this global death lead, Democrat Hilary Clinton tweeted that "Trump did promise America First."

Implying that America was first ahead of the global virus infections. She soon came under attack on social media by many including Democrat support-ers for the first time ever for using the dead as her political ploy in joking about the US leading in virus cases.

To further dampen the President's winning COVID-19 strategies, the WHO released the most frightening COVID-19 mortality rate of 14.6%. (14 deaths to 1000 infections).

Tedros later announced that the death rate for the coronavirus was 3.4%. In February, Doctor Anthony Fauci, director of the National Institute of Allergy and Infectious Diseases, said it was 2%.

Call it a hunch but President Trump immediately corrected the experts on March 4th by stating that even their 'overall case fatality proportion closer to 3.4%was 'really a false number' and that the actual mortality death rate to the num-ber of infections ought to be 'under 1%– this clearly showed the President was getting multiple advice and information from other very senior virologist experts.

This correction was scoffed at by the BBC, with disparaging remarks of the President having delusions of a medical background and implored on the view-ers to ignore the President and rely on the experts.

By May 26th, the CDC's latest 'Best Estimate' of COVID death rate was lower than the initial WHO claim. This estimate is usually calculated by divid-ing the number of known deaths by the number of confirmed cases.

This does not mean that the President or any of the others who predicted this are doctors or epidemiologists – quite simply, the President has an understanding of how statistics work. He knew that, in the early days of the virus, with limited testing and limited data, the numbers were going to seem a lot higher than they actually were and also, the more numbers are tested, the more the numbers of infection numbers.

The WHO were very reckless in announcing their data to the already terri-fied people without providing a simple explanation of the lack of sufficient test data – or perhaps the mainstream media vomiting what they are paid to say.

TESTING HOAX

Although Obama had halted all swine flu testing in the middle of the 2009 H1N1 pandemic and decided to forego testing and tracking individual cases because the media agreed that 'why waste resources testing for H1N1 flu when the government has already confirmed there's an epidemic?'

Some public health officials privately disagreed with the decision to stop testing and counting.

Reader, the media is owned by corporates within the Democratic Party. Their business interests were more important than people's lives and all the mainstream media totally buried this news – I too did not know about the 2009 H1N1 pandemic until I started re-searching for this book.

Back to 2020, the experts had advised that testing people would determine whether to tighten or relax social distancing measures, know who has been infected and the areas to focus on, in order to target resources and allow the health service to plan for demands for intensive care units. The blood test looks for signs of a previous COVID-19 infection.

Most important of all, if people have recovered from the virus, many will know when to get back to work if they had been self-isolating and provide antibodies.

The test looks for signs of a previous COVID-19 infection, which will help understand the pervasiveness and how widespread the COVID-19 had mutated within the communities. The leaks to the press began with Tedros commenting that

---

"We cannot stop this pandemic if we do not know who is infected."

Next, Anthony Fauci informed Congress that, "People cannot get tests for the coronavirus easily and that the US testing system is not meeting the country's needs."

That was rather vague scientific language to the man on the street including myself. However, we all understood that testing was not possible. The mainstream media and the Democrats loved this leak. The attacks on the Trump administration would not stop for days.

All the tests kits ordered from China were inadequate, they could only identify immunity in people who had been severely ill and not people that had slight symptoms.

The fiasco was even worse in the UK. Two Chinese companies were

offering a risky take it or leave or leave it proposition for two million home test kits at least $20 million. The asking price was high, the technology was unproven and the money had to be paid upfront. We were required to pick up the crate loads of test kits from a facility in China, and when the kits arrived around April 12th, all the tests ordered from China could only identify immunity accurately in people who had been severely ill and not people that had slight symptoms.

In effect, the millions of Chinese 'off the shelf kits' were a waste of time and money. And the kits that did work gave inconclusive results. The whole UK consignment still remains in storage unused.

The media and the Democrats soon got wind of the faulty test kits from China they got so excited that the American citizens had been conned by both the WHO and China, without putting out any suggestions or efforts to calm the people, they unleashed a barrage of insults – they were 14 hours too late little did they know that in the next 24 hours after the news was leaked, the country would be flooded with testing kits – the President had ordered US companies to begin manufacturing US made test kits two weeks earlier, as soon as he was advised that there was a problem with the test kits. The US was soon selling off the masks to the world.

TESTING FOR THE 2009 H1N1

In contrast, here is how Obama covered up testing in order to lie to the American people about the number of Americans that were infected. He hid the vast numbers from the American people that had voted them into office. The numbers of infected were as a result of improved testing. Having flooded the US with test kits, millions of people were now being tested. The Democrats were even aware of this because even in 2013, Obama had ordered halting tests during the pandemic in order to deceive the people and leave them in the dark.

As hypocritical as the Democrats could be, or perhaps, convinced that the people, especially the black people would forget, Joe Biden attacked the President saying,

"...the crisis in Arizona is the direct result of Donald Trump's failure to lead and his desire to "slow the testing down", and Americans are suffering the consequences."

Biden specifically called for the White House to,

"...immediately resume operating federally-managed community-based testing around the country and establish multiple sites...speed up the testing" nationwide ...putting politics ahead of the safety and economic well-being of the American people."

However, during the 2009 swine flu pandemic, Obama had suddenly told states to shut down their testing, without providing much in the way of explanation. And Biden's top advisor at the time had acknowledged that the Obama administration did not do "anything right" to combat the 2009 H1N1 pandemic. The reasons given were, "...why waste resources testing for the 2009 H1N1 flu when the government has already confirmed there's an epidemic."

Many health experts had disagreed with the corrupt deceptive Obama administration at the time but did not get the backing of the media.61 million Americans were infected, many died, all ages affected similarly but there was no media outrage, no lockdown, because there was cooperation with the Republicans to fight the enemy and to save lives.

As of today, the United States has conducted more than 66 million coronavirus tests. Our country is now averaging more than 800,000 tests per day and nearly 5 million per week. Trump was absolutely correct when he said that more coronavirus testing leads to more cases it's common sense that the liberal media fail to comprehend. This level of testing capability enabled the country to manage detected cases and reopen the economy safely at the same time.

DEATH WITH OR DEATH FROM COVID-19 HOAX

The statistics were still not quite accurate and this was because of how the figures were counted – it was a matter of 'death with' or 'death from' issue, both of which served to inflate the figures.

Death with coronavirus meant that a person could die from being run over-on death, may have been infected or may even be asymptomatic.

Death from coronavirus would include as it should, however, most of the patients had pre-existing health issues and naturally lower immune systems, which meant that they either died.

The figures over the weeks also meant that if a person died of any other illness, such as a stroke or even dementia, but had a touch of COVID-19 – that death was signed off as COVID-19, which inflated the number of COVID-19 deaths and would deflate and reduce the deaths by dementia and stroke.

By the end of March, Trump had flooded the country with testing kits and as such, the number of confirmed cases in the US had skyrocketed and by April 2nd, the US had outpaced both China and Italy in reported cases.

So, when the Coronavirus Task Force reported around April 7th that the infection rate had peaked and the curve was beginning to flatten, Trump tweeted,

---

"... The Federal Government is doing an excellent job. When they say the death toll isn't going to be as high as reported, they (the opposition) act like they're sad because it's lower."

A funeral director in Williston Park, NY, stated that every director expressed his or her concern that coronavirus deaths are being inflated and every death in NYC is being recorded as a COVID death with or without testing to confirm.

"Basically, every death certificate that comes across our desk now has COVID-19 on it."

A spokesperson for Schafer Funeral Home stated that, "They are putting COVID on a lot of death certificates because people who are going to their hospital with any kind of respiratory distress, respiratory problems, pneumonia, the flu — the flu-like symptoms lead into the COVID-19.

"To me, all you're doing is padding the statistics. You're putting people on that have COVID-19 even if they didn't have it. You're making the death rate for New York City a lot higher than it should be."

The true statistics and number of the virus in the states holds some concerns of exaggerations as most of the hospitals, if not all the hospitals in the Democrat run states began over counting COVID-19 cases in order to extort funding by labelling 'causes of death as Coronavirus'.

The numbers were including the statistics of people dying of other causes. The inflated numbers meant that if someone died from being run over by a tractor and also tested positive for having the virus – the person would be counted as a COVID-19 death.

There was another scandal in New York. More Than 40% of US Coronavirus deaths are linked to nursing homes. On July 23, 2020, at least 59,000 residents and workers died from the coronavirus at nursing homes and other long-term care facilities for older adults in the United States, according to a New York Times database.

As of July 23rd, the virus has infected more than 335,000 people at some 15,000 facilities. Almost 85% of deaths in NYC were from nursing homes while the elderly vulnerable residents make up only 0.5% of the population.

Nursing home populations were at a high risk of being infected and COVID-19, was particularly lethal to adults in their 60s and older who have underlying health conditions.

Following the CDC advice, Governor Cuomo had issued an order forcing several nursing homes to take in infected patients being released from the larger hospitals.

It was explained that the reason for this was for nursing homes to be set up as halfway point to returning home, however, he had overlooked that the patients were infectious and lethal to many uninfected residents.

Furthermore, Cuomo had followed the CDC advice that allowed nursing home staff who were COVID-19 positive to return to work right away if they were asymptomatic, not realizing that asymptomatic persons may be contagious, and that the elderly are most at risk of severe disease and death if they contracted COVID-19. One facility had to hire a refrigerator truck to hold all the bodies.

Note that the median COVID-19 death age is 78. As life span in the US is 78 years old – they were probably going to be dead anyway.

All mortality from CDC coded as Death with and not death from COVID-19, meaning CDC does not have the data of people that contracted it and died from it. Until July 2020, CDC still do not have the data can I explain further; quite well 3 weeks ago with no respiratory issues or health issues, went to Church – fell ill and died of COVID-19 within three weeks. Ensuring 'never let a serious crisis go to waste' for November 2020.

The world experienced a lethal pandemic 2009 H1N1 the Republicans worked with the Democrats to keep the people safe, with the least disruption in contrast, in order to impose their globalisation socialist lifestyle on all, including states that had very minimal infections, the mainstream media and the Democrats imposed;

- You should not go to church
- You should not go to school
- You should not go to work
- You should not go to the beach
- You should not vote in person
- You should not attend loved ones funeral
- You should not play college football
- BUT YOU CAN RIOT, PILLAGE AND DEVASTATE COMMUNITIES FOR SEVERAL MONTHS WITHOUT SOCIAL DISTANCING.

14

THE US LOCKDOWN

Until the lockdown, Trump was not able to display his leadership prowess. Undeniable, he carried on with keeping his campaign promises, most of which were conveniently ignored by the media and hidden from the people, especially the US minorities, which unfortunately included most of my very own friends and family and even myself until I decided to write this book. Everyone experienced the total lockdown of the workplace and schools, however, when funds continued coming into the peoples' pockets – because of the lifesaving decisive actions taken by the President, it all began to hit most of them that something (Trump) was happening in their lives. All of which was becoming more and more obvious on a daily basis, not only in the US, but globally.

Apart from the obvious health concerns, some countries, including France, Australia and Japan were making plans to evacuate their citizens from Wuhan. The Chinese had advised the WHO director to announce that, "unless we're convinced it's uncontrollable, why (would) we call it a pandemic?"

That comment fired up the Democrats who were relentless in attacking Trump for being racist and xenophobic for of his travel restrictions ban of January 17th and they were to use the lockdown to their personal advantage, to tank the economy and to ensure that the people remained unemployed.

The Trump administration declared a Public Health Emergency on January 31st, then on February 2nd implemented a ban of most foreign nationals who had recently travelled to China.

The WHO had argued that declaring a pandemic was politically fraught because it would lead to more drastic travel and trade restrictions, and stigmatize people coming from affected regions. It was obvious to many experts that it was now a pandemic, but they could not understand why Tedros was resisting taking the appropriate actions.

President Trump went even further and declared a National Emergency on March 13th, which allowed the federal government to tap up to $50 billion in emergency relief funds and relaxed the various strict regulations that were stifling the provision of health-care in order to speed up testing.

Within a matter of weeks, officials in Italy, Iran, and South Korea went from reporting single new cases to hundreds. There were no apologies from the mainstream media or the democrats for calling the President racist and xenophobic after his unyielding determination to order the travel ban from China.

That line of attack immediately ended – the democrats needed another angle to attack – to lockdown the country which would have the effect of tanking the economy and leaving at least 20 million people out of work, which Trump had insisted would be re-election promise.

The US and UK began shutting down and encouraging people to work from home around March 9th with an almost lockdown by March 13th when all schools were shut down, to be resumed at a later date in the future.

The 'lockdown' led to the Great Coronavirus Crash as the President had feared, with such a frightening speed and breadth – and quite unlike the 1987 crash that was caused by an imbalance in balance sheets, this was a life-and-death struggle with a microscopic enemy. The global impact led the Americans and the whole world to take the lockdown as a pandemic cause and not a Trump cause much to the disappointment of the democrats. Now they needed another scheme.

WE CAN'T LET THE CURE BE WORSE THAN THE DISEASE ITSEL

Due to the US federal system, each state had its own lockdown rules and the President had begun advising citizens at the end of February to stay home, and by the end of March, 32 out of 50 states had locked down.

The highly infected cities seemed to mostly be the ones that insisted on having "sanctuary cities". They had an influx of more people who were sleeping in the streets, on other people's property or just sleeping rough. Washington state started with so many illnesses and had more deaths, followed by California and New York.

The weeks before the end of March 'lockdown' saw the obsession with shopping and in particular, the hoarding of toilet paper. As in the UK, most of the grocery stores were laid bare in preparation for the lockdown.

Toilet paper became the ultimate symbol of panic buying around the coronavirus weeks. Companies that supplied it were stunned and had to adjust to the rapidly evolving new normal in consumer behaviour.

The US President immediately took leadership action to calm the situation by assuring that the truckers were still on the roads to stock up the shelves and that there were no shortages in addition. Thanks to the media and Democrats, few people believed the assurances and the fighting to grab toilet paper and hand sanitisers continued out of the stores and into the streets. The assurances mirrored the advice given to the hoarders here in the UK during the daily briefings with Johnson our Prime Minister.

On March 23rd, the President signed an executive order to prevent hoarding and price increases of supplies amid the coronavirus outbreak Since the coronavirus outbreak escalated in the US, there have been runs on hand sanitizer, toilet paper, bleach wipes, meat and canned soup, among other long-life cupboard products. People attempted to sell cleaning products and other supplies at inflated prices online on Amazon, eBay, and other sites which made White House trade adviser

Peter Navarro to send out a warning,

"If you got any large quantities of material that this country needs right now, get them to market or get them to us, we'll pay you a fair price. But if you don't do that, we're going to come for you."

As the lockdown creeped into the Easter Holy week, the President then stated that he hoped that churches would get "packed" from coast to coast, "I think on Easter Sunday, you'll have packed churches all over our country, I think it would be a beautiful time. And it's just about the timeline, I think is right," he said in an inter-view with Fox News.

The President, whose conservative political base is, in part, composed of millions of conservative Christians, had called the religious holiday a "special" day for him personally.

Of course both the Democrats and the media were triggered and foaming in the mouth because they felt it was too soon, they needed the country in lockdown and the economy destroyed, although there were few or no cases of the infections in most of the Republican states – they wanted the whole country to remain in lockdown – the media cleverly hid the fact that during the Obama's 2009 H1N1 pandemic, there was no lockdown, no masks, high death fatality but cooperation from the Republicans to flatten the pandemic curve.

The Democrats then called in Fauchi to provide an expert contradiction to Trump's statement – just to mock and humiliate Trump. In his response, Doctor Fauchi did not address the Easter timeline specifically, but stated that it might be possible for parts of the country to return to normal function while other areas combat outbreaks.

With the world markets in turmoil and with people in the US people losing their jobs by the thousands, the President was concerned about the people and commented that, "...the cure cannot be worse (by far) than the problem!"

I remember the statement that the President made on March 23rd, with an almost biblical prediction and exactly two months after the lockdown, over 500 doctors signed a letter telling the President that the shutdown was a mass casualty event because;

- Many Americans face evictions from their homes
- Rent had gone unpaid
- Depression from job losses as organisations
- Fear from the pandemic, baited on by the mainstream media
- Over 150,000 Americans each month had to cancel routine cancer screening checks
- Millions had missed routine dental care to fix problems strongly linked to heart disease and death
- The impact was more severe for disadvantaged children and their families, causing interrupted learning, compromised nutrition, and consequent economic cost to families who could not work

- Preventable cases of stroke, heart attack, and child abuse were on the rise
- Suicide hotline phone calls had increased by 600%
- Sales of alcohol had increased 300-600%, cigarette sales have increased
- Obsessive compulsive disorder (OCD) and hoarding of food mostly toilet paper and cleaning materials
- Family relationships have become frayed
- Millions of children's routine check-ups had been missed.
- Several experts stated that children were more likely to be harmed by not returning to school than if they caught the virus

In effect, poverty and financial uncertainty were closely linked to poor health, and many more health issues were now directly associated with the lockdown.

That was the however, the Democrats and the legacy media resorted to analysing it, and concluded that,

---

"Send people back to work without the outbreak under control, and you make it worse. Cases surge, hospitals get overwhelmed, people die, and states and cities come down with even harsher measures."

Trump was more practical and stated on April 15th, two days after Easter that, "the latest data has "put us in a very strong position" to reopen parts of the country."

That was his strategy to begin opening up the states. It must be pointed out that it was such a coincidence that the parts of the country with the greatest outbreaks were all Democrat-controlled areas.

Several months later, it was reported on May 4th that a shadowing pandemic of mental illness was emerging, and there was about a 1.6% increase in the suicide rate.

Records confirmed that 120,000 die every year from suicide and drug over does each year, however, 1.3 million were projected to die in the US from the coronavirus.

As the President tried to gradually open up the country from two days after Easter, about 80% of the Democrat controlled states remained shut down.

These states are predominantly run down, populated with black ethnic minorities and have suffered adversely not only from being run by democrats but from the pandemic.

A week after Easter had seen sparks of protests as many people were keen to get back since some areas were not affected by the virus. Most important of all, the statistics for the rest of the country had shown that the curve had peaked and infections were going down.

Many Democrats had projected that the coronavirus lockdown measures should be in place for six months – to September 2020 and had not anticipated the curve beginning to taper off so soon.

Even Doctor Tedros of the WHO official was to comment that,

"President Trump is doing a great job combating the coronavirus. He's doing all he can, that kind of leadership is very, very important."

I came across a rather interesting study by a Doctor Ayyadurai, a world-renowned systems scientist that rejected the response model pushed by Doctor Anthony Fauci.

Doctor Ayyadurai explained that it is not the virus corona-virus or otherwise that harms individuals, but a person's own faulty immune system.

He claimed that in healthy individuals, the impact of infections on people with a strong natural immune system would be mild and non-lethal; however, in those who are immune-compromised with weak immune systems such as the elderly and those with pre-existing conditions like heart disease, diabetes, or obesity, may lead to hospitalization and mortality.

Healthy adults may at most, experience a brief fever and flu-like symptoms, while cases of affliction in children are rare.

Confirming that all mortality from CDC coded as Death with and not Death from COVID-19, meaning CDC does not have the data of people that contracted it and died from it.

Many experts agree with Doctor Ayyadurai that it was not necessary to quarantine everyone, because the risk is the result of a weakened immune system, the key is to strengthen people's immunity which could be helped by Vitamin A supplements and Foods rich in sources of Vitamin A.

DIRECT DECISIVE ACTIONS

$8.3 BILLION EMERGENCY CORONAVIRUS SPENDING PACKAGE

On March 6th, the President was to sign $2.5 billion in order to upgrade the outdated coronavirus processes and for research to quickly produce a vaccine for the deadly disease, as the Coronavirus Preparedness and Response Supplemental Appropriations Act, 2020.

Initially, the President had intended to ask for more and to use unspent budget funds for the package and needed an urgent approval, but the Democrats had rejected that request, saying that existing money shouldn't be used to fight the virus.

They were keen on tanking the economy and obtaining funds to fund mostly organisations directly linked to their interests, which they did by vamping up the emergency bill to $8.3 billion. They had expected a haggling match but the President was later to state, "So, we're signing the $8.3 billion. "I asked for $2.5 billion and I got $8.3 billion, and I'll take it."

The $8.3 billion aid package sailed through the House and Senate. The size of the bill dwarfed the $2.5 billion in funding the Trump administration had originally proposed.

$2 TRILLION CORONAVIRUS AID, RELIEF, AND ECONOMIC SECURITY ACT (CARES ACT)

Initially, Trump had put forward $1.3 trillion dollars for the coronavirus economy stimulus – Speaker Pelosi demanded $8 trillion merely to bankrupt the country, use the black people as collateral damage and fund Democrat run organisations. She was in fact saying,

"The coronavirus would be a tremendous opportunity to restructure things to fit our vision."

The Coronavirus Aid, Relief, and Economic Security Act, also known as the Cares Act, is a $2.2 trillion economic stimulus bill passed.

The Treasury Secretary Steve Mnuchin had warned on March 21st 2020, that millions of people may have to stay home until June 2020 in order to slow the spread of the coronavirus.

Combined with actions undertaken by the Federal Reserve and the administration, Mnuchin proposed a bill that would have a $2 trillion net impact on the US economy, with nearly 1 in 4 Americans, or 80 million having to close up shop and stay home to try to curb the spread of the coronavirus.

Little did they know that the President had planned on firing a few inspector generals that had been in office since Obama's administration.

Pelosi had insisted on the additional $5.8 trillion to fund non corona virus related projects such as;

- abortion clinics,
- renovating arts galleries,
- Funding to make airlines lower carbon emissions etc.

All of which had nothing to do with helping the Americans to survive the impact of the pandemic and would not have done much to jump-start the economy.

This $2.2 trillion US stimulus package is the largest emergency relief bill in American history. The bill plans to help people, families, businesses, and the economy cope with the disastrous effects of the COVID-19 pandemic. The President eventually got $2.2 trillion and immediately set off to plan B. He immediately got rid of seen Inspector Generals, and appointed new ones, who in addition to their other duties, included keeping management informed of fraud, abuses, and deficiencies.

In addition, their roles ensured effective supervising, in preventing and detecting fraud and abuse in its programs and operations, in order to control the billions of dollars in federal funding from the coronavirus stimulus bill.

Part of the Cares Act is the The Paycheck Protection Program (PPP). The $669-billion business loan program was set up to directly help certain businesses, self-employed workers, sole proprietors, certain non-profit organizations, and tribal businesses to continue paying their workers and help the economy reopen more smoothly.

$2 TRILLION (£1.7 TRILLION) CORONAVIRUS AID BILL ECONOMIC PACKAGE

On March 26th, the US Senate passed the $2 trillion (£1.7 trillion) coronavirus aid bill, the largest economic stimulus in US history to help cushion the effects from the coronavirus lockdown on the Americans.

Prior to this, the bill hit several blockages including one from the Republicans who argued that the unemployment funds were 'a strong incentive for employees to be laid off instead of going to work' – they further stated that they would oppose the bill unless it was fixed to ensure workers could not have a higher income while unemployed than in a job.

The day before the bill was signed, the day was marked with furious debate on the Senate floor, as Republicans accused House Democrats of proposing an alternative stimulus bill that was full of unnecessary progressive wish-list items.

Senate Democrats in the meantime repeatedly blocked the Republican's stimulus bill.

After the final amendments were made to satisfy the objections, the plan eventually included;

- Direct payments of $1,200 to most American adults and aid to help small businesses pay workers
- Direct payments of $1,200 to millions of individuals who earn $75,000 or less, and an additional $500 per each child
- An expansion of unemployment aid including payments, to self-employed persons that may also work in the gig economy
- A $500 billion fund to help companies, which included loans to hard-hit sectors such as the airline industry
- $350 billion in loans for small businesses
- $100 billion for hospitals and related health systems on the frontlines of the pandemic

Spurred on by the media and her supporters, before the bill was passed, Nancy Pelosi, had blocked Trump's original $1.3 trillion stimulus bill, despite over 17,000,000 Americans having lost their jobs from the pandemic by insisting on an exhaustive list of unnecessary non-COVID-19 related demands. Her ridiculous list had included;

- $25 million to the Kennedy Art Center that she had personal interests in.
- Funding for Same-day voter registration,
- Funding for voting by mail
- The expansion of wind and solar tax credits.
- Funding for refugees overseas
- Automatic extension of non-immigrant visas.
- $4 billion in emergency funds to equip and protect the New York museums.
- $350 million for refugee resettlement and allocated
- $25 million for "salaries and expenses" for the House.
- While death numbers were horrifying the world and governments were scouring for life saving respirators and masks to curb the death toll and save lives, the Democrats were insisting of adding to the death toll by demanding funding for Planned Parenthood the top abortion providers.

LET THEM EAT MY STASH OF ICE CREAM

Prior to agreeing on the bill, the Democrats continued to hold off agreeing on the Presidents' coronavirus relief fund well into April 16th, 2020. The people suffered during this period, and in her keenness to show off her hateful stubbornness, House Speaker Nancy Pelosi let her guard down and was interviewed eating and showing off her ice cream collection and well-stocked royalty-class refrigerator on national television.

Social media erupted in dismay and disgust for Pelosi for delaying the bill and for adding on the non-coronavirus related items while the American people suffered.

There were comments like:

- "While Nancy Pelosi sits in her ivory tower in San Francisco, snacking on her $100 a gallon ice cream out of her $24,000 fridge, she is cheering on Democrats for blocking coronavirus relief aid."

- "My husband hates Trump and said after they blocked the stimulus deal today, he will vote anything but Democrat in the election. So, thanks Pelosi you literally lost one of Trump's biggest critics today when three years of debating with me wouldn't budge him at all, 'I think yesterday was a red pill for a lot of people."

- "I am a Republican and not a huge Trump fan but seeing how the Democrats are handling themselves during this crisis is scary and disgusting."

- "Me too. I support Trump since the impeachment hokes."

- "We welcome you and your husband with open arms. I was a Dem for seventeen years prior to President Trump running. All my best to your family."

Trump was asked about the questionable expenditure of $25 million allocated to the Kennedy Center for Performing Arts in D.C; his response was,

---

"The Kennedy Center has suffered greatly because nobody can go there, it's essentially closed, and they do need some funding. And I said, "Look- that was a Democrat request." That was not my request. But you got to give them something. It's something that they wanted. You know, it works that way."

2020 RIOTING

In the Democrats' mantra 'never to let a serious crisis go to waste' especially when the black race is involved, barely a few days from May 25th 2020, in their continuous quest to tank the economy, the sparks of rioting flared up.

The rioters were locking people inside their homes, arresting business owners, and destroying the economy. They said it was necessary, they said,

---

"Millions of Americans would die from COVID-19 if we didn't step in line, close our doors."

But, those very same Democrat leaders were now out in the streets, surrounded by masses of people, marching in the Floyd protests, with most with neither masks nor social distancing.

The racial chaos in the United States following the killing of George Floyd brought much to light. At the very least, it showed normal folks just how anti-American and morally-fetid the Democrats had become and as George Soros paid and encouraged the mainstream media to loop the storyline of the death of George Floyd for weeks which had now become an attack on the President.

In the days following the racial upheaval, many millionaires had not bothered to de-escalate the rhetoric that had been driving anger, and they had even stoked the tensions because it was financially expedient for them. Trump haters like Meghan Markel, Snoop Dogg and various other celebrities took the opportunity to attack President Trump and weaponized the killing to convince millions of the dangerous propaganda that America's systems, aided by the police are actually racists and there was a need called to 'defund the police'.

George Floyd, had died a few hours later, following the most horrific knee restraining method by the police.

The Democrats could not leave a disaster go to waste; the gruesome death of George Floyd played directly into their race hate agenda. Soros came into the fore and paid and sponsored protestors mainly the Black Lives Matter group and Antifa to get out on the streets to riot. The eight weeks lockdown and feeling of 'guilt for being white' added on the swell fanned by the media.

Several people had died during the protest, indiscriminate burning and destruction of businesses, pillaging and fighting on the streets of the mainly Democrat run cities, however, George Floyd's killing was broadcast over and over again by the mainstream media, and was followed by the reporters' commentaries of race hate.

The protests and anarchy soon reached the UK – the protesters decided to burn properties, looting became rife with desecration of grave stones, the vandalism of plaques and pulling down of statues.

Despite lockdown measures still being in place across much of the country, many commentators stated that the rioting indirectly meant that the lockdown was over or that the experts were directly biased for leaving the rioting yet forbidding people from attending Sunday masses or funerals of loved ones.

The protests in Minneapolis in response to police killing was claimed to be the largest public US demonstration over police brutality since the onset of the pandemic.

The President was aware that the riot and unnecessarily excessive media goading were targeted at him, but maintained his usual time bidding. The more he ignored them, the more the upped their goading to painting of the streets yellow with the wordings 'Black lives matter' and arson attacks on Roman Catholic Churches – seen by many to be a direct attack on the FLOTUS, a staunch Roman Catholic.

The experts soon warned that the riots that flared after the death of George Floyd could hamper the effort to curb the virus, with concerns that the protests were breeding grounds for the spread of the virus as many protesters did not wear masks and many who covered their faces could not possibly have protected themselves from the virus despite doing so.

Even the peaceful non-violent protests sadly in only Democrat run black communities involved many higher-risk groups on the streets – which made the experts concerned that the coronavirus may even spike.

The people were influenced into accepting that the way forward is venting hate, burning the US flags, seeing the country fail, churches burnt, businesses vandalised and looted just to spite the President for exposing and seeking to improve the corrupt states that they live in, instead of being left to implode.

Black Lives Matter movement continued to burn down and destroy mostly America's black neighbourhood run by the Democrats and none of the Democrats, not even Pelosi condemned their actions.

And just like that the rioting stopped the coronavirus lockdown which ended the historic battle with the invisible enemy as the economy gradually opened up with very little resistance from the media.

15

OPERATION WARP SPEED

Key part of managing COVID-19 was trying to decrease and delay the epidemic peak, known as "flattening the curve" the point that the infection peaks, levels out and in fact, begins to fall.

This is done by slowing the infection rate, using all the lockdown guidelines, in particular social distancing, to decrease the risk of health services being overwhelmed, allowing for better treatment of current cases, and delaying additional cases until effective treatments or a vaccine becomes available.

Fauchi and others have been at pains to emphasize that the President's suspension of direct flights from China on January 31st and from Europe on March 11th had saved a large number of American lives, in contrast to Presidential candidate Joe Biden and Senate Minority Leader Chuck Schumer calling the suspension of flights from China 'Hysterical, xenophobic and racist.'

Disease Expert continued to state that 'herd immunity' is the only way to defeat the virus without a vaccine and that if all that was required was to flatten the curve was through social distancing and masks, deaths or severe cases would not be prevented. You just change the dates and that the only two ways to deal with the virus are to develop a vaccine a process that could easily take a year at best or build the nation's herd immunity by weaning people off of most restrictions currently in place.

Some people question why the current coronavirus has brought the world to standstill while a previous deadly coronavirus, SARS, did not.

Others have questioned why a vaccine is so urgently needed now to stop the spread of the current coronavirus when a vaccine was never developed for

SARS, while the March 2003 virus was aggressive and lethal and patients typically showed symptoms within two to three days unlike COVID-19 that provided at least four.

The Democrats needed the lockdown to impede the elections and punish the people – through debts or mental illness. For now, only Trump's optimistic statements have propped up the Dow Jones and assured the people that things will get better soon. He had tweeted on March 25th;

"The real people want to get back to work ASAP. We will be stronger than ever before!"

At a coronavirus task force briefing, Trump declared that

"The country was nearing the end of our historic battle with the invisible enemy of coronavirus."

Trump's approval numbers have hit their highest point ever since he re-opened the economy and by the end of April, 69% of Americans approved of his handling of coronavirus against 31% who did not.

HYDROXYCHLOROQUINE & AZITHROMYCIN

A debate about hydroxychloroquine was sparked around March 13th after President Trump touted the drug as a possible "game-changer" in the fight against the COVID-19 pandemic, prompting critics to accuse him of peddling unproven, untested remedies.

At a press conference, he needed to assure the world and talked about various options which included hydroxyl chloroquine' and then concluded, "What do you have to lose?"

What happened next was a global demand for the medication and praise for the President. The Democrats did not want a cure, and not as early as April at that, they would rather the people died off, the following coronavirus briefing saw Doctor Fauchi being hurled into the furore. Doctor Fauchi was forced to admit that, "The medication is only anecdotal."

Taking their cue from the mainstream media, the WHO commented that, "to date, there is no evidence that any medicine can prevent or cure the disease."

Many even stated that it was dangerous to take. However, an international poll of thousands of doctors rated the Trump-touted anti-malaria drug hydroxychloroquine the best treatment for the novel coronavirus.

Outside the US, hydroxychloroquine was equally used for diagnosed patients with mild to severe symptoms whereas in the US, it was most commonly used only for high risk diagnosed patients, the survey found.

The medicine was most widely used in Spain, where 72% of physicians said they had prescribed it.

During the survey, a total of 6,227 physicians were questioned in thirty countries about at least fifteen treatments used for COVID-19.

Of the 2,171 doctors asked which drug was most effective, 37% said hydroxychloroquine. By contrast, 32% answered "nothing."

MECHANICAL VENTILATION

When COVID-19 first began to spread, governments across the world didn't have much of a clue as to what the best treatment would be.

The experts had stated that only oxygen provided by the ventilators were the only best-known treatment.

Being the most informed person in the country, the President was aware of the problem with ventilators, which doctors were reporting high death rates for COVID-19 patients on ventilators, leading some to question whether they should be used at all and the various other options that could be tried, such as using treatments for other corona related disease.

Mechanical ventilation always comes with risks: a tube must be placed into a patient's airway to deliver oxygen to their body and this invasive form of support, meant that up to half of patients sick enough to require this type of ventilation did not make it. And 80% of the patients on ventilators died.

ANECDOTAL CURE OF HYDROXYCHLOROQUINE

Here he meant it that their claims were not necessarily reliable because the cure varied from individuals to individuals rather than on scientific facts. For instance, a headache can be cured with only one aspirin for 'A', but may require two tablets every four hours for two days for 'B'.

Many other experts were not accepting any form of treatment and hoped instead on a new vaccination that was probably not going to be ready for trials in six months to two years. The anti-Trump corporate media loved the conflicting opinions between the experts and the President and ferociously leapt into action to discredit him. CNN ran an analysis piece with the headline: 'Trump Peddles Unsubstantiated Hope In Dark Times.;

Others followed: '

He was giving "false hope" to people infected with COVID-19.'

'Trump's Dangerous Messaging about a Possible Coronavirus Treatment.'

'The Meaning of Donald Trump's Coronavirus Quackery.'

The tipping point was when 'Democrat' lawmaker State Representative Karen Whitsett, who was infected with the coronavirus credited President Donald Trump and his advocacy of 'hydroxychloroquine' with saving her life, and various news of people who had been cured began trickling in.

Fox News' political commentator Tucker Carlson with his colleague Laura Ingraham, were some of the first media personalities in the US to bring on guests claiming that the antimalarial drugs hydroxychloroquine and azithromycin were helping people infected with the virus.

On March 21st, another credible person that was diagnosed with coronavirus claimed that he was saved from certain death by the anti-malaria drug. Giardinieri, the vice President of a company that manufactures cooking equipment for high-end restaurants in Los Angeles, said he had three doses of the medicine and is hoping to be discharged from the hospital within five days,

---

"I was given Benadryl and some other drugs and when I woke up around 4:45 a.m., it was like nothing ever happened."

Hydroxychloroquine, is a prescription drug that has been used to treat malaria for decades and auto-immune diseases like lupus.

Overseas studies have found it to be promising as a treatment for COVID-19, though it hasn't been approved by health officials.

FACEBOOK AND TWITTER POLICING ANECDOTAL CURE POSTS

During a press briefing in May, a reporter had asked the President whether he would take the drug – which was widely reported as deadly; despite being in use for over forty years.

The President immediately responded that he was taking a course which started three days previously.

Other countries continued deploying the anti-malarial drugs in various settings.

Brazil even relaxed its restrictions on the drugs to allow doctors to prescribe them to patients with mild coronavirus symptoms, not just those in a serious condition in hospital.

President Bukele of El Salvador has said he and 'other world leaders' were also taking it.

Brazilian President Jair Bolsonaro claimed in a video that 'hydroxychloroquine is working in all places', but his statement was removed by Facebook for breaching its misinformation guidelines.

Undeterred, around March 19th, the President decided to order the FDA to fast-track the testing of hydroxychloroquine and Azithromycin as treatment for COVID-19 for the drug to be made immediately available to coronavirus patients, the malaria drug that had shown potential in battling other coronavirus, which will be able to reduce the severity or duration of the symptoms.

By the end of April, it was confirmed that when used at the early stages of infections, Hydroxychloroquine & Azithromycin was effective the press immediately stopped that angle of attack – no apologies to the President.

It was even reported that 58 nursing home patients in the US were treated with 92% success, and a Veterans Affairs Study and showed that it actually demonstrated the effectiveness of hydroxychloroquine, especially when combined with azithromycin.

But on April 24th, the FDA issued a warning about the dangers of using the substances because of reports of heart rhythm problems in patients and then on July 3rd, 2020, New York Governor Andrew Cuomo spoke positively of the antimalarial drug hydroxychloroquine which has been touted by the White House at his daily press briefing, announcing that the state will request an additional supply from the federal government. The President's most vocal hater said that 'the drug has anecdotally been effective' in treating COVID-19.

Explaining that state officials have been given permission to use it in combination with the antibiotic Zithromax in hospitals 'at their discretion'. However, he emphasized that official data has not yet been released.

"There has been anecdotal evidence that it is promising; that's why we're going ahead."

Governor Andrew Cuomo also pointed out that some patients are unable to take hydroxychloroquine due to their pre-existing conditions or medication regimens.

The President was right all along; zinc prevents the duplication of the virus in the cell, and the hydroxychloroquine increases zinc uptake by the cell. Doctors who use the two in combination were reporting spectacular results that the media and the Democrats continued to hide so as not to give credit to the President.

A viral video showed several doctors confirming that they had cured COVID-19 patients using hydroxyl chloroquine. It featured a Doctor Stella Immanuel, an Afro American physician from Houston, Texas, speaking on the steps of the US Capitol in Washington, surrounded by several other doctors, hailing hydroxychloroquine as a "cure".

The Houston doctor also dismissed mounting evidence that face masks substantially help limit the spread of coronavirus.

Three months later, the 'anecdotal' cure controversy still would not rest. On July 24th 2020, Twitter limited some of Donald Trump Junior's account, after the President's eldest son shared claims about the anti-malaria drug hydroxyl chloroquine as a coronavirus treatment.

With Twitter and Facebook policing tactics, I can just imagine British telecom, our UK phone company cancelling my account because they do not like what my friends and I talk about.

VACCINATIONS

Several conspiracy theories have been spreading on social media against the uses of vaccinations as a cure for COVID-19. Several people including Judy Anne Mikovits, the American anti-vaccination activist formerly at Whittemore Peterson Institute (WPI) are not very keen either.

She now claims that from her studies and experiments, she does not believe that a vaccine is needed to prevent COVID-19, and claims that the coronavirus was "caused by a bad strain of flu vaccine that was circulating between 2013 and 2015." She also claimed that,

---

"Masks will "activate" the virus and re-infect a mask-wearer over and over and that the global health system uses vaccines merely as weapons to make profits."

Judy Ann also made claims that Doctor Anthony Fauchi had sabotaged her research. After Judy Mikovits' reports were fact-checked by experts, they claimed that her study is either false or not based on evidence.

Doctor Mikovits also made statements about the methods used for counting COVID-19 deaths. Her claims mirrored other experts' claims, for example, if one died in a motor accident, but tests positive with the COVID-19 virus, the death would be recorded as a COVID-19 death; this method of collating the figures highly inflated the numbers people that die of COVID-19. As such, the figures released by the US and UK provided considerably exaggerated death numbers from the COVID-19 pandemic.

OPERATION WARP SPEED

This was one of President Trump's most important responses to the coronavirus, a historic partnership between the federal government, scientific community, and private sector to develop a safe COVID-19 vaccine in record time.

The Trump vaccine, WARP Speed, provided up to $2.1 billion to Sanofi and GlaxoSmithKline to fund development and manufacturing of the' experimental COVID-19 vaccine, to provide the US with 100 million doses of the vaccine, which will begin human trials in September 2020. As with other vaccines in development, the Sanofi-GSK vaccine, if effective, would require two doses.

Novel vaccines usually take about six to ten years but Trump got it to trial in record six months.

This vaccine required new platforms because the experts claimed that COVID-19 was not like SARS or H1N1.

Many people have recognised the President's leadership especially in handling the issues related to COVID-19. Even CNN Anchor John King stunned liberal colleague host Erin Burnett on the programme "OutFront" when he declared that Trump was right on COVID-19 leadership and suspending funding to WHO, in response to Trump's announcement that he was suspending funding for the WHO — pending an investigation into its handling of the coronavirus pandemic.

The President continued to show undaunted incredible leadership over the pandemic. The media was still very relentless and spent so much time trying to destroy him and quite like the democrats would not work together to help the people.

No other President has been known to deal with so much open hostility and animosity while achieving so much success.

Despite the economic crash, COVID-19 was beginning to be in Trump's favour looking at how pandemics have affected elections in the past, a trajectory which the Democratic voters probably don't know usually favours the sitting President.

Excitement of Trump's electoral doom is at best premature. At worst, the coronavirus will certainly impact the election, but there are more factors.

Most Republicans and Democrats have seen the full impact of having key manufacturing abroad, and the part that the Chinese played in hiding data from the world, and the election may well play out in play to be based on who is best placed to handle the Chinese.

16

CHEAT-BY-MAIL DEMOCRATS LAST BASTION

The logical notion here is that, if people can go out to relax in the parks, go out to buy their food, go out to put fuel in their cars – all for just about being outdoors for about two hours can well stand in the queue (line) for up to around fifteen minutes to vote in person.

VOTER ID

Many people have stated that the only way that President Trump may fail to get re-elected in November 2020 would come from Ballot fraud. Trump knew this and as soon as the democrat's announced their strategy for email voting, social media went into a frenzy and someone actually tweeted that if Hilary can delete thousands of emails and the FBI had let her get away it – there is no telling on what could happen to the email votes. Although absentee Ballots are a great way to vote for the many senior citizens, military, and others who can't get to the polls on Election Day, this has been open to fraud. Several people have been caught posting ballot cards with names of deceased persons. Also, the argument has been raised that if people can go out on the streets to riot in the heat of the coronavirus pandemic for several hours, then they can go out to vote and queue up for only 10 to 30 minutes.

Several interesting viral memes read,

"Prevent Trump Voter Fraud – Get Voter ID"
"If you can protest, you can Go Out to Vote."

In the last Presidential election, 35.5 million voters requested absentee ballots, but only 27.9 million absentee votes were counted, according to a study by Charles Stewart III, a political scientist at the Massachusetts Institute of Technology.

He calculated that 3.9 million ballots requested by voters never reached them; that another 2.9 million ballots received by voters did not make it back to election officials; and that election officials rejected 800,000 ballots, which statistically suggests an overall failure rate of as much as 21%.

He continued that, "If 20%, or even 10%, of voters who stood in line on Election Day were turned away, there would be national outrage."

As going to the polls to vote requires standing in close proximity to other people, the Democrats are determined to mandate nationwide vote by mail. And they want the ballots to be mailed out automatically to everyone whose name is listed in the voter registry, whether they request one or not and whether they are dead or alive. There is so much potential for mischief here that this process could more accurately be described as "cheat-by-mail."

The US Election Assistance Commission and the Election Administration and Voting Surveys reveal that 16.4 million ballots mailed to registered voters went missing between the 2016 and 2018 elections.

Since 2012 a staggering total of 28.4 million ballots have gone missing. That's 28.4 million opportunities to cheat. The irony is that the democrats yet refuse to mandate Voter ID – clearly sending out 'cheat to win' tactics such as used in developing countries to enable them to exploit their citizens.

Whatever suppressive effect the pandemic might have on voter turnout it's believable that the pandemic will have the complete opposite effect that the Liberals are hoping for and it may hand Trump a second term.

However, according to the New York Post, it seems as if some of Washington's top Democrats had a similar view as the President in 2004, when House Judiciary

Committee Chairman Jerry Nadler also argued that he believed that mail-in voting is "susceptible to fraud."

VOTE BY MAIL

Democrats are not letting the coronavirus crisis go to waste politically. As Trumps fights this global war and hidden enemy, they are using the global pandemic to provide moral cover for their 'Vote By Mail' scheme, which they hope to implement nationally to replace in-person voting at polling places.

Many are concerned about the 'Vote by Mail' bill introduced by Democrat Senators. Ron Wyden and Amy Klobuchar could result in all Americans using postal voting in November. If the bill does not survive a potential Trump veto, Democrats are sure to continue agitating at the state level to get Vote by Mail laws before November 2020.

In early April 2020, several hundreds of illegal voter cards were found in several States. And many have equally commented that if people can queue at their grocery stores for an average of 20 to comply with social distancing – why can't they queue to vote.

The Black Live Matter (BLM) protests supported by the Democrats also served to support that argument. As thousands of lawless anarchists rampaged through the main US cities without regard to social distancing and not bothering to wear masksthe Democrat's argument for 'Vote by Mail' dismally failed.

BALLOT FRAUD

Some people will use the terms absentee ballots and mail-in ballots are two different methods of voting instead of queuing (lining) up to vote in person.

Absentee ballots specifically refer to ballots that are mailed when a person can't vote in person, and the term mail-in ballots is in the context of voting policies that enable all people to vote by mail.

Some people have begun to abuse the system for voter fraud and in fact, several politicians have been convicted.

Absentee ballot fraud is the most common and the most expensive to investigate and can never be reversed after an election.

BALLOT HARVESTING

Another concern is ballot collecting, also called ballot harvesting. This is characterized by the gathering and submitting of absentee or mail-in voter ballots by third-party individuals, volunteers or workers, rather than submission by the voters themselves directly to ballot collection sites.

Note that caregivers, friends and family members may collect and submit ballots however, this too has the potential for fraud with the collector's intentions, as they may be motivated not to deliver the ballot once they collected it, especially if they are of a different political party than the voter, or in a desperate attempt simply break open the mail boxes or collude with the post office sorting office, as raised in the President's tweet,

"There is NO WAY (ZERO!) that Mail-In Ballots will be anything less than substantially fraudulent. Mail boxes will be robbed, ballots will be forged and even illegally printed out and fraudulently signed…"

MAIL-IN ELECTION FRAUD

Several people over the decades have been arrested for election fraud crimes – the most recent was in July 2020, authorities arrested and charged four Democrat officials over a mail-in election fraud scheme in New Jersey, proving President Donald Trump's concerns over vote-by-mail to be right. Criminal charges against the four individuals including Paterson City Councilman Michael Jackson and Councilman-elect Alex Mendez were filed by New Jersey Attorney General Gurbir S. Grewal for allegedly engaging in voter fraud with mail-in ballots.

The investigation was launched after hundreds of mail-in ballots were found bundled together in a mailbox in Paterson.

Realistically, mail-in voting serves two purposes, the protracted delays of months of investigations after the elections, before releasing the results, especially in the swing states and vote rigging.

The Democrats have exhausted every possible scheme to stop the President from being re-elected. Their very last barricade and final blockade is a proposal to expand mail voting so that people standing in the queues for ten minutes to twenty minutes may not contract COVID-19, while it is alright to riot for hours without social distancing honestly!

17

CONCLUSION

This November 2020 looms even closer, the democrats have exhausted most of their schemes to endanger the lives of the Americans and destroy the economy, all of which President Trump has managed to counter with the help of his powerful cabinet and his leadership and decisive actions in handling COVID-19.

The great president Trump will also be remembered for his policies and how successfully implemented them despite the barrage of fake news attacks by the mainstream media and dispelling the Democrats' only policy and flippant accusation of 'racist' in their belief that only the black votes would shield and continue their corrupt past.

The unprecedented COVID-19 was a new experience for all including the experts and when looked at from the timeline perspective we see that the president took the reins early on and acted on saving millions of lives in contrast to the Democrats and mainstream media that downplayed the crisis.

The President has remained selflessly unhinged in carrying out international and national policies on behalf of his American people to the world as reflected by the cues followed by other countries in combatting the pandemic – President Trump has consistently put the health of all Americans first. The media in the UK did not report about the peace in the Middle East that no other president ever achieved nor even thought ever possible, the first time ever in a quarter of a century. President Trump has remarkably advanced peace in the Middle East and formally normalized diplomatic relations between the Arab nations and Israel; and some of my friends have asked what has Trump ever accomplished to motivate me to not only writing a book about the president but to give it that title here again I do not blame them for being so ignorant, they only listen to the biased main stream media.

As quite a few of the opposing Democrats politicians and mainstream media reporters are openly beginning to declare the President's leadership and decisive actions taken, the president may have succeeded in returning bi-partisan, reconciliatory politics to the people which may well serve to unite the divided people. Many people are not so keen about their 'undermine and destroy' policies with their 'never to let a serious crisis go to waste' mantra. Despite all of that, the great president has stormed on with his negotiations and deals and the previously tanked economy is showing very good recovery rates, so has the employment figures.

If Trump pulls this off, he would have silenced the democrats including Obama, who had tweeted that the pre pandemic economic boom had begun at his watch as early as 2012 with a clean slate.

Many Trump supporters have concluded that 'bad boy Trump' is no longer that billionaire businessman, TV celebrity, but one that cares about one thing doing the best for America and all Americans.

- He warned about protecting the Southern borders which saved millions of lives from the pandemic.
- He told the Americans that he wanted to bring manufacturing back home.
- He told the world to be less dependent on other countries
- Most important of all, he warned the world about China.
- Like a train, he never stops delivering and not just talking about his policies.

Democrats offer a $4 trillion taxation on peoples' salaries, reestablishing stronger manufacturing ties and affiliations with China, held up releasing the August 2020 stimulus funds to help the American people by overplaying their hands in negotiating with their demands of amnesty to 11 million illegal immigrants and prisoners, with free education and health to all immigrants thus bribing them for the Democrat votes and playing politics that had nothing to do with the pandemic while people-orientated Trump released four counter emergency

Executive Orders to pay out and help the people to cope during the hard times, instead of Pelosi's fixation on re-establishing business affiliations with China. As American economy begins to recover, even a former Obama adviser predicted that by November, "The election may well become a referendum on which candidate – Trump or Biden – is most trusted to be tough on China."

In March, just before the lockdown, the US unemployment rate was hovering near historic lows at 3.5%, with 127.98 fully employed.

Around At the end of July 2020 despite the shutdown it was at 121.2 million. With three months to go, the great President Trump seems to be surpassing expectations.

President Trump has literally continued to carry out his policies and campaign promises to Make America Great Again and promote global peace has not stopped. Democrats and the evil media attacked him every step of the way and it is no longer about November 2020, the choice is simple, there is no other choice, the silent majority have seen to that– it now seems that the focus should be 2024.

ACKNOWLEDGMENTS

To the negative left leaning media – BBC, ITV, Sky and LBC. If they were not very nasty, I would not have had much to write about

COMING SOON

THE PEOPLES PRESIDENT

BY
MARIE OTIGBA